CONTENTS

TIFFANY FRANCIS

FOOD
YOU CAN
FORAGE

EDIBLE PLANTS TO HARVEST, COOK AND ENJOY

BLOOMSBURY WILDLIFE

LONDON · OXFORD · NEW YORK · NEW DELHI · SYDNEY

To my lovely family and to Dave

'The sight of the awful and majestic in nature had indeed always the effect of solemnising
my mind and causing me to forget the passing cares of life.'
Mary Shelley

BLOOMSBURY WILDLIFE
Bloomsbury Publishing Plc
50 Bedford Square, London, WC1B 3DP, UK

BLOOMSBURY, BLOOMSBURY WILDLIFE and the Diana logo are trademarks of
Bloomsbury Publishing Plc

First published in Great Britain 2018

A catalogue record for this book is available from the British Library

ISBN: PB: 978-1-4729-4120-6; ePDF: 978-1-4729-4118-3; eBook: 978-1-4729-4119-0

2 4 6 8 10 9 7 5 3 1

Design by Gridlock Design
Printed in China by C&C Offset Printing Co., Ltd.

To find out more about our authors and books visit www.bloomsbury.com and sign up for our newsletters

**To ensure your own safety and to protect the environment, please refer to page 7 for information
on the ethics and safety of foraging.**

AN INTRODUCTION TO FORAGING

When I was writing this book, I was asked countless times by friends and family to explain exactly what foraging was. Most knew it involved gathering fruit from the hedgerows and seeking out the first wild garlic leaves of spring, but I was also asked if I'd be scrumping pears from private orchards (no comment) or scooping up roadkill for a hot pot (no ethical objection here except my vegetarianism). I think, foraging is one of the most fascinating and enjoyable hobbies there is and one anybody can get stuck into – from the tiddliest child to that bizarre friend of yours who can't tolerate dirt. For me, foraging means learning about the wild plants in your local environment, gathering the edible ones and eating them in the most satisfying way possible. It's about collecting edible treasures from our native trees and simmering them into dark, sticky jams, and about biting on the earthy crunch of hazelnuts fresh from the husk, tasting the salt crystals hidden in a frond of seaweed, and gathering silver mushrooms under a sky scattered with stars.

The art of foraging is almost as ancient as humanity itself. One of the first adaptations early humans made was the transition to hunting and gathering. We taught ourselves to hunt wild animals and gather plants to feed our families, habits that became so essential to our survival that it lasted for 90 per cent of human history, before farming was introduced at the end of the Stone Age. In a world before online shopping and takeaway pizza, foraging was a vital part of daily life

for our ancestors and one on which they depended to stay alive. Now we have such secure, affordable and varied food production, why should we bother to forage for our food? Why seek out blackberries, hazelnuts or thyme when we can find them all in the vegetable aisle?

By examining how far we have strayed from our primordial roots, it becomes more and more apparent why we must reconnect with nature and our wild origins. In Stephen Moss' 2012 Natural Childhood report for the National Trust, it was revealed that on average, British children watch more than 17 hours of television a week and spend more than 20 hours a week online. While there are positive benefits of screen time, the belief is that children are not being given the freedom to escape outdoors and enjoy the natural world. Access to nature has also proven to have positive effects on the mental and physical health of adults. It is essential that we switch up our weekly schedules and spend more time in the beautiful landscapes our country has to offer – foraging is the perfect way to do it.

We are also living in a world where more and more people are keen to know where their food has come from. Cheap products with dodgy labels are all very well, but many of us now rightly insist on understanding the provenance of our food, particularly regarding animal welfare, environmental costs and unethical ingredients.

When carried out sustainably and respectfully, foraging is an incredibly environmentally friendly choice, as there is no reliance on chemicals and pesticides, the food is seasonal, and there is no carbon footprint from importing and transportation. It can literally be harvested fresh from the ground and carried lovingly to your own kitchen, ready to be savoured and devoured. When I scoop a thick blob of blackberry jam onto a piece of warm toast, my mind fills with recollections of misty autumn walks and the kitchen cupboard is transformed into a scrapbook of delicious memories.

THE ETHICS AND SAFETY OF FORAGING

A good forager is an ethical one. Pick only the amounts you need to ensure plant populations remain healthy and leave plenty for the birds and wildlife with whom we share our wild food. Remember to keep to public places and steer clear of private land, as it is illegal to trespass or forage there without permission. You don't need any snazzy equipment to forage, but I tend to bring a Thermos of tea, Tupperware tubs, scissors, gardening gloves and a raincoat.

Think carefully about the places you want to forage. The countryside is full of delicious wild food, but avoid searching along the edges of large agricultural fields which have often been treated with chemicals. Similarly, watch out for popular dog walking routes where our canine companions may have kindly marked their territory. As a general rule, if a patch of plants looks particularly shrivelled or unhealthy, it's best to leave it alone.

My favourite thing about foraging is the thrill of a new species, but remember the golden rule: If you're not 100 per cent sure, don't pick it. There are plenty of extra resources online that can help you feel more confident with identification, and social media is a fantastic place to ask others for help. This rule is particularly important for mushroom picking, for obvious reasons; as with all wild fungi, eat only a small, cooked amount of new species if you haven't tried them before. There are surprisingly few deadly species of fungi in Britain, but plenty can give you a dodgy belly. Pregnant women should also be careful of certain species like bog myrtle and chamomile; it's always best to take extra care and consult your doctor if you're unsure.

MAKING GOOD USE OF THIS BOOK

As with all outdoor experiences, the most important aspect of foraging is being in the natural world and overloading your senses with the sights and sounds of nature. With that in mind, this book is a springboard guide to understanding which plants and mushrooms are edible, where to find them, which season and how to harvest them. It's a loyal and friendly companion for afternoon walks, coastal excursions and days out with the family and should provide enough information for you to start understanding more about our plants and how delicious they can be. Whether you've paused for a cup of tea or just need a photograph of a particular berry, this book contains everything you need to start foraging and develop a great new hobby. It also includes information on the wildlife you might discover, accompanied by my helpful illustrations, plus historical facts, mythology, literature and folklore, as well as my collection of recipes for you to try at home. Enjoy!

INTRODUCING WOODLAND

When you consider how much woodland fills the green spaces of Britain, it comes as no surprise how deeply trees have carved their way into British folklore. From Robin Hood's lair in Sherwood Forest to Shakespeare's moonlit realm in *A Midsummer Night's Dream*, our forests are alive with ancient stories and myths. They can be dark and dangerous, full of bears and witches waiting to eat each other up, or places of delight, where you might meet elves or be raised by a family of wolves. Either way, it's worth the risk for a taste of what grows within.

When William the Conqueror commissioned the *Domesday Book* in 1086, a 'great survey' of the land to understand 'how it was occupied, and by what sort of men', the area of land covered by woodland had reached 15 per cent. Since that time, changes in land use, industry and population have seen the destruction of some woodland, but thanks to charities like the Woodland Trust, thousands of acres of new trees are planted each year, and forests still cover 13 per cent of the land.

Protecting our forests isn't just important for the plants and creatures that live inside. In 2015, the Woodland Trust commissioned a report by Europe Economics to identify the economic benefits of woodland in Britain, which found that our trees are worth a staggering £270bn in today's economy. The simplest way to understand this figure is to look at their physical value; the sale of timber contributes £1.7bn to the economy and employs 14,000 people, and traditional woodland practices, like hazel coppicing, provide a sustainable source of material for the future. Trees also help to strengthen the ground beneath us, prevent floods, improve water quality and combat climate change by absorbing carbon from the atmosphere.

Aside from their physical value, modern research is demonstrating the benefit of woodland for

recreational purposes, physical activity and mental health. The trees are there to help us walk off that second helping of roast dinner, or to entertain our children for hours at no extra cost. We need our woodlands to walk the dog, ride mountain bikes, eat picnics and raise heartbeats, and reports show that people who suffer from anxiety, stress and depression can improve their mental health by spending time in green spaces like woodlands.

Most of us don't need statistics to recognise the value of British woodland. A walk beneath the trees is a delight in all seasons, from fresh April dawns dizzy with the aroma of wild garlic, to bright October afternoons in thick jumpers. The forest floor is always bustling with new plants and fungi; primroses, foxgloves, celandines and bluebells create a carpet of colour in the cool shade of the trees and mushrooms grow in every gloomy crevice. Look up, and the rest of the world is blocked out by bustling foliage; it's that raw, cosy solitude that can only be found in the depths of a dark forest.

The woods are a haven for flora and fauna alike and are the perfect place for an afternoon of foraging. Hiding in the leaf litter or dangling from the branches above, a vast array of edible plants are waiting to be harvested, squashed into Tupperwares and consumed. After the first green shoots start to arrive in spring, look for garlic mustard, sorrel, ground ivy and common valerian to add a wild twist to a side of vegetables. Summer brings mallow flowers and wild strawberries, wonderful for decorating cakes and bringing natural sweetness to your kitchen. By autumn, most of the fungi have developed on the ground and rotting wood, and the trees will be heavy with juicy berries; keep an eye out for hawthorn, elder and blackberries to make sure you grab a few before the birds gobble them all up.

HAWTHORN

CRATAEGUS MONOGYNA September to November

According to Celtic lore, haw berries make a tremendous remedy for a broken heart. For those not so tragically afflicted, they are also one of the most abundant hedgerow berries to use in the kitchen. Look out for bustling clusters of fruits in pillar-box red, spread across the country in woodlands, downland, heaths and parkland. The hawthorn is one of many flora that produce a 'Mayflower' as in this month the shrub blossoms with white flowers speckled with pink and black anthers. Like the blackthorn, hawthorn trees are covered in sharp spines up to an inch long and the leaves are 2-5cm long with three to seven lobes.

While a little too dry to eat raw, the berries are one of the key ingredients in hedgerow jelly as they are naturally high in pectin and set easily. As a general rule their large seeds make them difficult to use whole, but they can be infused in vinegar to produce a tangy condiment, or used to make tea and cordial. Young leaves in spring have a delicate flavour and can be chopped and added to potato salad.

Hawthorn
Vinegar
page 234

ELDER

SAMBUCUS NIGRA June and September to October

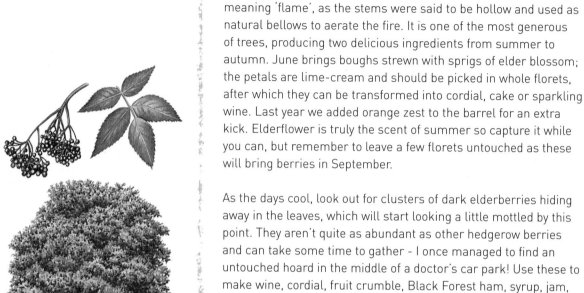

The elder tree takes its name from the Anglo-Saxon word 'aeld', meaning 'flame', as the stems were said to be hollow and used as natural bellows to aerate the fire. It is one of the most generous of trees, producing two delicious ingredients from summer to autumn. June brings boughs strewn with sprigs of elder blossom; the petals are lime-cream and should be picked in whole florets, after which they can be transformed into cordial, cake or sparkling wine. Last year we added orange zest to the barrel for an extra kick. Elderflower is truly the scent of summer so capture it while you can, but remember to leave a few florets untouched as these will bring berries in September.

As the days cool, look out for clusters of dark elderberries hiding away in the leaves, which will start looking a little mottled by this point. They aren't quite as abundant as other hedgerow berries and can take some time to gather - I once managed to find an untouched hoard in the middle of a doctor's car park! Use these to make wine, cordial, fruit crumble, Black Forest ham, syrup, jam, chutney or my favourite, spiced elderberry buns with lemon icing. The elder tree grows across Britain and particularly around rabbit warrens, where their seeds are easily distributed in droppings. Leaves are pinnate with toothed leaflets.

Spiced Elderberry Buns
page 236

BLACKBERRY or BRAMBLE

RUBUS FRUTICOSUS August to October

The bramble is undoubtedly one of the more cantankerous of shrubs, skulking behind garden sheds and hooking onto bootlaces mid-step. In summer the stems blossom with pink and white flowers, a pretty reminder of colder months ahead when plump, dark berries will sit between the thorns, ready to take centre stage in a hot crumble. When I was little, my mum and I would go scrumping for blackberries, cooking apples, pears and wild plums and concoct delicious autumn puddings in the kitchen. When the last of the berries disappear the bramble once again lies quiet, adorned with frost and spiderwebs. Look out for the dewberry (*Rubus caesius*) which looks almost exactly the same but tastes even better; you may never know which species you've stumbled upon.

Found in hedgerows, woodland, heath and scrub across Britain, the berries themselves are a cluster of small fleshy segments each containing one seed. They first grow green and then red, before turning very dark purple. The stems are prickly with toothed, pinnate leaves. There is some old country rule about not picking blackberries after the first frost because you may get mixed up with the devil somehow, but with the changing climate I find the best harvest time can shift annually. If September and October have been particularly mild, you may even find berries until Halloween. Early fruits are sweeter and can be eaten raw off the twig; use the rest for pies, jams, syrups, wine and infused vinegar.

Blackberry
& Pear
Crumble
page 246

Blackberry
& Basil
Syrup
page 218

WILD STRAWBERRY

FRAGARIA VESCA June to August

This little flavour bomb grows throughout Britain, but especially on chalky soil like the South Downs, where I live, in Hampshire. It's easy to miss wild strawberries if you're not staring intently at the ground, but suddenly through the grass you'll find hiding an explosion of bright red berries and it's difficult to resist an immediate gorging session. Small and deliciously sweet, I've found large batches on grassy banks and in weed-smothered pits in the ground, but they can also be found in woodlands, scrub and limestone exposures. They are particularly recognisable from their tiny flowers, five white petals around a lemon centre, as well as coarsely toothed leaves up to 6cm long.

The flavour of wild strawberry is much more intense than the domesticated variety, but they are small and don't tend to grow in large volumes. They are delicious raw, but can also be added to crumble, cake, ice cream, vinegar, jelly, jam and as an accompaniment to sparkling wine. You can also make a supreme strawberry vodka by steeping the berries in vodka and adding sugar.

LESSER BURDOCK

ARCTIUM MINUS May to July

A common and plentiful plant, many are familiar with burdock because of its tendency to leave thick, spiky burrs in the coats of furry dogs. My old golden retriever Murphy had fur like velcro and we would spend many afternoons teasing burrs from a blonde forest of fluff. In other cultures the burdock boasts a less irritating reputation; native Hawaiians claimed that it aided strength and endurance and sought after the plant during difficult tasks. In Britain, the burdock plant grows in scrub and woodland thickets except in the very north of Scotland. Stems are tinted red and the leaves are large and heart-shaped. The burr fruits look like reddish-purple pom-poms surrounded by a cluster of hooked bracts.

Young leaves make a delicious substitute for spinach, while the stems can be steamed and buttered like asparagus tips. The root can be peeled, boiled and sautéed as a tasty side dish, but can also be combined with dandelion and carragheen to make an aromatic beer. Alternatively, blend dandelion, burdock and hawthorn flavours to create a delicate tea infusion. It is also a popular ingredient in Japanese cuisine, who call it 'gobo' and add it to miso soup and other dishes as a body purifier.

SWEET CHESTNUT

CASTANEA SATIVA October to November

I always love exploring the scientific names of plants and animals; I feel they reveal a little more about their cultural history. Not surprisingly, *Castaneis* is the Latin word for chestnut and the hispanic instruments castanets are so called because they are traditionally made of hard chestnut wood. The sweet chestnut is a familiar childhood tree, producing hedgehog-like cases filled with red-brown nuts that fall to the floor in their hundreds. They are found in most woodlands and parks across Britain, with purplish-grey bark and long leaves with toothed edges. It's not to be confused with the horse chestnut or conker tree, which produces hard knobbly cases and isn't edible.

The nuts are usually best found in the grass, but if you'd like to gather them straight from the hedgehog, simply stand on the cases and they should pop open if they're ready. I love eating them raw but they aren't to everyone's taste as they can be dry and contain tannins. They are marvellous roasted – particularly over a fire – or they can be boiled, peeled and eaten with sprouts or pureed for use in soups, stews and stuffing. They also make a fantastic chocolate and chestnut log cake for Christmas!

WALNUT

JUGLANS REGIA October to November

The botanical name *Juglans regia* means the 'royal nut of Jupiter' and takes its name from the Roman god who is thought to have lived solely on walnuts when visiting earth. It's no surprise he loved them; they're my favourite nut too (I've always enjoyed their resemblance to miniature brains) and are much desired by squirrels and other mammals. Walnut trees are common in the south (but become rarer further north) and can be found in woodlands, parks and gardens. With smooth, greyish bark and pinnate oval leaflets, the walnut itself is hidden inside a shiny green capsule, which splits open to reveal its crinkled treasure in late autumn.

While these tempting pods start to appear as early as June, it's best to wait until at least October to harvest the nuts when they're mature and hardened. Beware of the juice in their shells which will stain everything brown and store collected nuts in a cool place until use. They make a fantastic and healthy treat raw, or use them to make coffee cake, bread, stilton tarts, granola, or to decorate a handsome cheeseboard.

OAK

QUERCUS ROBUR October to November

There are many countries in which the oak tree holds regal status. In Britain, it has become a metonym for traditional carpentry and sturdy English mannerisms, but it's also a keystone species in woodland ecosystems and provides essential nourishment and shelter for birds, mammals and insects, including the purple hairstreak butterfly. Fallen acorns become important treasures on childhood walks and every year I find them buried in my allotment beds by opportunistic squirrels. The oak tree is found throughout Britain, instantly recognisable by its oval leaves with four to five rounded lobes on each side – think of the National Trust logo! The acorn fruit can grow up to 4cm long and rests in a scaly cup.

Like sweet chestnuts, acorns contain tannins which can make them unbearably bitter if not prepared correctly. Try burying them in the ground over winter to allow the tannins to leach out; they will be sweeter and more digestible and can be roasted and ground to make an alternative to coffee once popular in wartime. My brother-in-law also makes an excellent oak leaf rum; simply infuse oak leaves in cheap rum to encourage a darker flavour.

LIME

TILIA X VULGARIS June to July

The lime tree is a familiar site in urban areas, particularly along streets and avenues as they make excellent shaded walkways. Found throughout Britain in parks, gardens and woodlands, it is traditionally used to make happy-tappy Morris dancing sticks, but bees will also swarm around the fragrant flowers due to their honeydew. The tree itself is tall and domed, while the leaves are broad and oval-shaped with a finely toothed margin. Flowers are creamy with five petals and the nut is thick-shelled.

Gather the flowers from late June to July, when they are in full bloom and smell the most divine. Lay them out to dry in a warm place for two to three weeks, before using to make linden tea, a beverage that dates back to the Middle Ages. This is served without milk and is renowned for its delicious taste and soothing properties regarding the nervous system and anxiety. For an extra tang, add fresh elderflowers to the brew to create a breezy summer infusion.

Pesto Primavera
page 224

GARLIC MUSTARD

ALLIARIA PETIOLATA March to April

Known to rural folk as Jack-by-the-Hedge due to its tendency to grow along hedgerows, garlic mustard is always easy to spot alongside other woodland flora. Its foliage is bright green (the colour of peas fresh from the pod) and sprinkled across the plant tops are small white flowers. The leaves are distinctly toothed and wavy and the stem rises high above other plants with few extended branches. Garlic mustard can be found throughout Britain in woodland, scrub and chalky pastures and, unsurprisingly, archaeology has revealed it to be one of the oldest herbs used specifically for cooking across Europe.

The entire plant is deliciously garlicky and emits a strong odour reminiscent of rustic kitchens. Historically it was recommended as a flavouring for salty fish, but it can also be used to make a sauce to accompany roast lamb. I tend to use it, together with nettles and wild garlic, to concoct a pungent pesto or to wrap fresh goat's cheese, much like Cornish Yarg. The leaves are best picked young to capture the flavour; fortunately, the aroma of garlic mustard lingers for a much shorter time than wild garlic or domestic bulbs, so is an excellent choice for social dining.

SORREL

RUMEX ACETOSA February to May

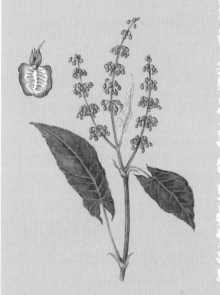

With a name that originates from the Old French word for sour, it's no wonder the taste of sorrel leaves has been likened to lemons, kiwi fruits and unripe strawberries. It can actually be found throughout most European countries and is a popular ingredient in a number of continental dishes: in Russia and the Ukraine sorrel is used to make a green soup called shchavel borscht and the famous Greek pastry spanakopita is traditionally filled with feta, leeks and sorrel leaves. In Britain, it is usually found in grasslands and woodland clearings on acidic soils and is particularly recognisable for its long, arrow-shaped leaves with backward-pointing lobes. In summer it produces rosy, coral-coloured flowers which attract small copper butterflies.

Sorrel leaves can be used as a wild substitute for spinach, in salads, soups, vegetable dishes or simply sautéed in butter on their own. They also make a fantastic accompaniment to oily fish and shellfish, particularly mackerel, scallops, mussels, herrings and salmon. For a tasty sauce, simmer crème fraîche, a dash of white wine and a squeeze of lemon, before adding young sorrel leaves.

JEWEL WEED

IMPATIENS CAPENSIS April to July

Also known as orange balsam, the jewel weed is a bright cantaloupe-coloured relative of Himalayan balsam, possibly the most infamous of invasive species. A native of North America, the orange balsam was introduced to England in the nineteenth century and has now naturalised throughout southern England and much of Europe. It can be found on riverbanks and woodland edges and grows up to 1.5m tall. Like its Tibetan cousin, the pods explode on the lightest impact, spreading their seeds to great distances, hence the traditional name 'Touch-Me-Not'. Stems are fleshy and almost translucent, with long, oval leaves that are pale and waxy underneath. The flowers are very beautiful, with five golden petals mottled with brown spots.

Young leaves and juicy stems make an excellent addition to fresh salads, or they can be steamed like spinach with other vegetables and tarted up with a little cider vinegar. Pre-explosion seed pods are great in stir-fries or eaten raw and bear a similar taste to walnuts; simply pop the pods over a container to release the seeds and use in the same way as poppy seeds.

COMMON MALLOW

MALVA SYLVESTRIS July to October

One of my favourite flowers to spot throughout the summer and autumn months, the mallow always pops up like somebody has dropped a bag of bonbons. Recognisable for its bright pink and purple colouring and pretty stripes, the colour mauve was actually named after the French word for this plant in 1859. Its sister plant the marshmallow (*Althaea officinalis*) has been used since Egyptian times to make what has today evolved into a squidgy pink sweet toasted over bonfires. In Britain, they are found on roadsides and waste ground, as well as woodlands and field margins across the country. The stem is thick and furry, with round leaves covered in soft down; the flowers have five mauve petals striped with purple lines.

Young leaves and shoots are juicy and excellent in salads, soups and stews. The flowers are perfect for crystallising and make a wonderful decoration for puddings, like my poppy seed and marmalade cake. Simply coat each flower with egg white and sprinkle with icing sugar, then leave to dry and solidify for a spectacularly sweet finish.

HAZEL

CORYLUS AVELLANA September to October

Lending its name to the lapine hero of *Watership Down*, the hazel tree is a common species found in both wild and coppiced woodlands. The branches are extremely flexible and have been used for thousands of years to weave into wattle fences. I work on an educational farm and the goats will do anything for a nibble of hazel leaf; we dangle branches into their paddock and call it 'goat-fishing'. The leaves are immediately recognisable for their heart shape, serrated edges and heavily lineated surface. Mustard-coloured catkins fill the canopy earlier in the year and by September the tree is laden with pale nuts encased in a crown-like husk.

While it may be tempting to pick them as soon as they appear, I've learnt from experience that trying to eat an unripe hazelnut will result in at least half an hour of chewing. On the other hand, you don't want to leave them to disappear into the paws of greedy squirrels. The best indication of ripeness is when the husk peels off easily or they fall to the ground. Delicious raw, they are also a fantastic addition to granola, salads, cranberry bread and fruit cake.

GOOSEGRASS

GALIUM APARINE All year

One of the most amusing plants to discover as a child, goosegrass (or 'sticky buds' as we called them) brightened up Sunday afternoon walks with the 'How many sticky buds can you attach to Mum's coat before she realises?' game. Their stickiness is due to thousands of tiny hooks on their leaves, stems and fruits, which are designed to cling to animal fur and assist with seed dispersal, although it seems small children perform the task just as well. The plant is actually from the same family as the coffee bean and can be found all year round throughout Britain, in hedges, woodlands and disturbed ground. They can reach 1.2m in height and tend to sprawl outwards to cover as much territory as possible. The leaves are narrow and oval-shaped, clustered in crowns of six to eight. Once the white flowers have transformed into little round fruits, they appear in pairs.

Try to gather young shoots and leaves before the seeds harden and they can be chopped and used in fresh salads or as an alternative to spinach in cooked vegetables. To make a less caffeinated coffee substitute, slow roast the seeds at a low temperature and grind them for use in a cafetiere.

COMFREY

SYMPHYTUM OFFICINALE March to May

A common plant in southern Britain, comfrey is most famous for its medicinal and horticultural uses rather than its role in the kitchen. It's very popular on allotments as a nutrient fixer in the soil (we have one planted under our apple tree) and the leaves can also be soaked in water for a few weeks to make a pungent but effective fertiliser. The leaves themselves are incredibly nutritious, being high in Vitamin A, riboflavin, potassium, manganese and fibre. Flowers blossom in spring to produce bell-shaped heads in a range of colours, from white to coral-pink or purple. In Britain, common comfrey is found across the south but can also be confused with Russian comfrey, a hybrid plant that is taller but still edible.

Comfrey leaves and shoots make an excellent addition to fresh salads or can be cooked with spinach and other vegetables. Stalks can be collected before the flowers blossom and eaten like asparagus, after blanching and steaming. It is also a popular leaf for herbal tea due to its sweetish flavour and many testify that comfrey leaves make wonderful 'leaf fritters', using pancake batter to transform them into tasty snacks.

COMMON VALERIAN

VALERIANA OFFICINALIS April to July

The valerian flower always seems to me like it belongs in a wedding bouquet rather than woodland soils; indeed, in medieval Sweden the heads were placed in a groom's wedding suit to ward off evil intentions from local älvor elves. The flowers themselves are pale pink and frothy and were used to make perfume in the fifteenth and sixteenth centuries, although their scent is a little Marmitesque and can be difficult to like. Found throughout Britain, the plant is stout with unbranched stems and pointy, toothed leaves.

Young leaves make a great addition to vegetable dishes but they can be bitter, so ensure they are fully boiled to produce a spinach-like flavour. The roots are popular for medicinal uses, especially for anxiety and encouraging sleepiness; one root can be infused in dark hot chocolate to create a sweet and soothing treat.

HERB BENNET

GEUM URBANUM May to July

Also known as the wood avens, this bright yellow flower grows in shady woodland spots and hedgerows across southern Britain and is pollinated heavily by bees. It is said to drive away evil woodland spirits and protect against rabid dogs. Medicinally, it is known as an antidote for snake bites – although I wouldn't completely rely on that. Seed dispersal is dependent on a much gentler process: the travelling rabbit. Like burdock, the fruits are surrounded by sticky hooks that bury themselves in the fur of small mammals and the laces of ramblers. The plant grows up to 60cm tall and flowers from May to August with five lemon-coloured petals; the leaves grow in threes and fives with toothed edges.

Young leaves should be picked when the flowers start to blossom and can be cooked like spinach or added to summer soups and stews. The roots have historically been used as a spice for soups and ales, due to their strong flavour similar to cloves. Try adding a peeled root with cinnamon, nutmeg and peppercorn to mulled cider at Christmas for a warm, aromatic tang.

WOODRUFF

GALIUM ODORATUM April to June

The Latin word *odoratum* ('perfumed') reveals the most famous property of this plant, known for its sweet smell that actually emboldens after drying. Also known as scented bedstraw or master of the woods, the leaves and petals emit the scent of vanilla when crushed and the entire plant has historically been dried and used for natural potpourri. It can grow to a quarter-metre in height and produces long, oval-shaped leaves with tiny prickles along the edges. The flowers are small and funnel-shaped, with four white petals around 5mm wide. Woodruff is mainly found in old woodlands full of history, particularly among beech trees on chalky soils throughout southern Britain.

The flavour of woodruff is very popular in Germany and is used to flavour juices, beer, brandy, jam, ice cream and herbal tea. It was traditionally used to flavour May-cups or May punch due to its sweet taste; nowadays it can be combined with borage flowers and added to cold Pimms in the summer months.

GROUND IVY

GLECHOMA HEDERACEA March to May

Historically named run-away-robin, field balm or creeping charlie, ground ivy is a common plant found in woodlands, hedges and grasslands throughout Britain. It is very popular with hungry bees due to its pale violet flowers that blossom in the spring and was traditionally used by the Saxons as a way to flavour, clarify and preserve beer before hops were discovered as an alternative. The plant appears to creep across the ground with reddish flowering stems and has kidney-shaped leaves up to two inches long, with toothed edges. The flowers are bilaterally symmetrical and appear in pairs.

While the leaves add a peppery punch to most dishes, try to collect them before the plant flowers in spring, as the taste can become rather bitter. It can be sautéed like spinach, added to vegetable soups and stuffings, or it can be added to herbal teas for a natural brew.

WILD GARLIC or RAMSONS

ALLIUM URSINUM March to June

In early spring the countryside is still recovering from the bitterness of winter and the first wild garlics to unfurl are a welcome harbinger of warmer days. The woodland almost swells with the unmistakable aroma of wild garlic plants, whose Latin name *ursinum* refers to the brown bear's habit of digging up their bulbs for a pungent snack. It can be found in woodlands, copses and other shady locations throughout Britain and the pointed, oval leaves can grow up to 25cm long. The flowers appear as beautiful creamy clusters in the undergrowth, creating a forest floor that seems almost sprinkled with stars. Due to their early blossoming time, they are a valuable source of nectar for butterflies, hoverflies and longhorn beetles. The flowers also help the forager distinguish wild garlic from other poisonous plants like lily of the valley, which can bear similar leaves.

Combined with nettles, wild garlic is the perfect ingredient for homemade pesto, which in turn can be used to liven up Italian dishes through spring and summer. It can generally be used in any dish that would usually contain garlic or spring onions, but be aware that wild garlic holds a milder flavour than the domesticated variety and quantities may have to be increased. The leaves also make a fantastic wrapping for homemade cheese, much like Cornish Yarg, as the garlicky flavour infuses into the cheese while providing a natural rind. My favourite use for wild garlic is to make warm cheese scones, oozing with flavour for a perfect afternoon treat.

Wild Garlic
& Cheese
Scones

page 212

PIGNUT

CONOPODIUM MAJUS May to August

Shakespeare must have thought highly of pignuts, as Caliban offers them to Stephano and Trinculo in a bid to secure their loyalty in The Tempest. Like truffles, pignuts are a favourite food of wild pigs, who snuffle into the soil to dig up the nutty root tuber. Found in meadows, pastures and woodlands on alkaline soils, the plant above ground is recognisable for its tall stems and white umbrella-shaped flowers. It can be difficult to follow the stem through the ground, as the tuber can sometimes be buried quite deep, but it's worth the effort as the nut itself tastes of earthy hazelnuts.

Once the root has been found, wash and peel it before eating it raw. It can also be boiled or roasted like chestnuts, or added to noodle soups with ginger and soy sauce.

SCARLET ELF CAP

SARCOSCYPHA COCCINEA January to April

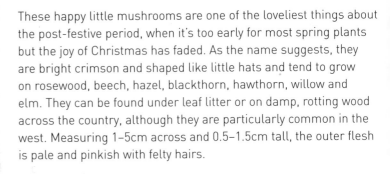

These happy little mushrooms are one of the loveliest things about the post-festive period, when it's too early for most spring plants but the joy of Christmas has faded. As the name suggests, they are bright crimson and shaped like little hats and tend to grow on rosewood, beech, hazel, blackthorn, hawthorn, willow and elm. They can be found under leaf litter or on damp, rotting wood across the country, although they are particularly common in the west. Measuring 1–5cm across and 0.5–1.5cm tall, the outer flesh is pale and pinkish with felty hairs.

Despite their pleasant, earthy flavour, scarlet elf caps are not favoured among gourmet chefs and are perhaps chosen mainly for their decorative quality. Nevertheless, I think they are worth foraging. The flavour is best captured by drying in the oven on a low setting, or they can be eaten fresh as a canapé – try filling with my homemade pesto using early wild garlic shoots.

GIANT PUFFBALL

CALVATIA GIGANTEA July to October

Found in fields, woodlands and under hedges on rich soils, giant puffballs are an unmistakable discovery. The body is ball-shaped, white and leathery with firm flesh throughout; this starts white when the fungus is young, but turns yellow and then rusty brown as it matures before the body breaks open and releases its spores. It's extremely important to only eat the puffball when the flesh is white, as the slightest yellow or brown colouring means it has matured too long and is now toxic. To identify whether the puffball is edible, slice it open and check the flesh inside is solid and pure white.

The flesh of a giant puffball is flavoursome with a satisfying texture much like a sponge cake. Cut into the body and ensure there is no yellowing flesh, then eat it fresh as there is no good way to preserve it for later use. Try scooping out the middle and frying it into a garlicky risotto, before returning it to the hollow body to serve.

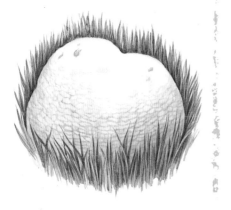

Puffball Risotto
page 228

HEDGEHOG FUNGUS OR URCHIN OF THE WOODS

HYDNUM REPANDUM June to November

With a smooth, creamy cap and short, thick stem, the hedgehog fungus is so named for its spore-bearing underbelly covered in darker spines. This chubby mushroom has no poisonous lookalikes and has a pleasant odour with soft, crumbly flesh that can taste a little bitter. The flavour is most intense when grown under a coniferous tree, but they can also be found in leaf litter in all woodlands and along mossy riverbanks, sometimes arranged in a fairy ring. The cap can reach 10cm in diameter, with a stem that's 2–6cm tall and 1.5–3cm thick.

While many choose to remove the spines on larger specimens, I find they are perfectly edible and add a little extra to the texture of a meal. Try slicing up and adding to meat or fish dishes, or preserve the fungus by slicing and drying at a low temperature in the oven. It can even be pickled in a jar with cider vinegar and capers for a tempting antipasti.

CAULIFLOWER FUNGUS

SPARASSIS CRISPA July to November

Also known as the brain fungus, this creamy white species is covered in ribbon-like curling branches that morph together to form a huge cauliflower shape. Found in coniferous woodlands at the base of pine, spruce and fir trees, they appear throughout Britain but are fairly uncommon. The flesh is distinguished for its meaty texture, sweet aroma and pleasant flavour. Like the giant puffball, the cauliflower fungus tastes best when creamy white, before it starts yellowing with maturity. They can grow up to two feet in width.

The best way to enjoy this unique fungus is the simplest; remove any dirt hidden in the ribbons, then fry with a little butter, sorrel and sea salt. After picking, the fungus can also be kept fresh for a few days by immersing the cut stem in refrigerated water. It can also be preserved by drying or being submerged in olive oil or cider vinegar.

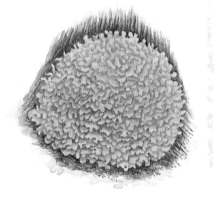

DRYAD'S SADDLE

POLYPORUS SQUAMOSUS July to November

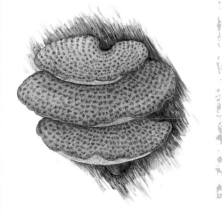

The name of this polypore fungus originates in Greek mythology, as it is believed the tree nymphs (known as dryads) could comfortably sit on top; it is also known as 'pheasant's back' due to the intricate markings on the bracket. Found on broad-leaved trees like beech, elm and sycamore, it tends to grow in clusters on logs, stumps and decaying trees throughout Britain. Measuring up to 60cm in width, the bracket is shaped like a half moon, anchored to the wood with a short, brown stem. The 'saddle' surface is brown to creamy yellow with bands of triangular scales, while the spore-bearing surface underneath is cream-coloured.

This species is best collected when young. The flesh is thick and leathery and the strong flavour makes it a great addition to soups, stews and casseroles. It dries well in the oven at a low temperature and can also be preserved under olive oil.

OYSTER MUSHROOM

PLEUROTUS OSTREATUS All year

These are lovely mushrooms that grow throughout Britain on stumps, trunks and fallen branches of deciduous trees like poplar and beech. They form in large, tight clusters, with a fruiting body that is convex when young, maturing into an oyster shell shape with a wavy margin. The cap varies from bluish-grey to brown or cream, with a white stem and thick, white flesh that bears a pleasant aroma and flavour. The Germans first cultivated this species during World War I when food was more scarce; it is now grown across the world and is particularly popular in Chinese, Japanese and Korean cuisine.

Like most mushrooms, the oyster is best collected when young to ensure optimum flavour. Remove the tough stems before cooking and add to dishes for a little meatiness. It also dries well and can be preserved under olive oil or cider vinegar.

WHAT'S IN A NAME?
THE ROOTS OF BOTANICAL WORDS

As all good gardeners and tree surgeons know, while every plant species has an official name and numerous nicknames, each species is also allocated a scientific name formed from Ancient Greek or Latin roots. Despite having rather insulting reputations as 'dead languages', Latin and Ancient Greek are extremely useful and the benefit of labelling every species in the world with a scientific name is simple. To the British, a buttercup is a buttercup, but to the Germans, that same buttercup is a *butterblume*, and to the Hungarians, it is known as *boglárka*. Just as mathematics is an international language, we use scientific names to determine a plant's identity no matter where it pops up. (The buttercup's genus is *Ranunculus*, Latin for 'little frog' as it tends to grow near water.)

Plants were labelled using Latin and Greek because the first people to ever record them accurately lived a long time ago. In the fourth century BC, the Greek philosopher Aristotle taught a student called Theophrastus, who devised a scientific terminology for plants after he inherited the botanic gardens of Athens. Theophrastus observed a number of features about each plant – such as their shape, habitat, fruit, leaves, bark and roots – and used his observations to create an individual name for identification. Before the untimely eruption of Vesuvius in AD 79, the Roman naturalist and philosopher Pliny the Elder used Theophrastus'

work to draw up an encyclopaedia called *Historia Naturalis*, which became the foundation for most of the plant names that we still use today.

Although I was fortunate enough to study Latin in school, I'm the first to admit my principal use of it has been at pub quizzes (one golden memory involved working out *digitalis* meant 'fingers', and therefore foxglove). However, as a literature student and lover of words, my knowledge of Latin has always proved extremely useful for working out how specific plants' names came to exist – something I find very satisfying! For example, the common poppy's name *Papaver rhoeas* refers to both the Latin *pappa* for 'milk' and the Greek *rhoeas* for 'red', while wild thyme's *Thymus serpyllum* originates from the Greek for 'creeping' due to its serpentine growth across the ground. Not only do these names transport us into the minds of those who created them millennia ago, but the names also help us to recognise and remember distinctive features of the plants we see around us. Here is a list of common scientific names found in British plants:

ALBUS The Latin word for 'white', usually used in reference to a species' appearance like *Chenopodium album* (fat hen) and *Lamium album* (white dead-nettle). An easy way to remember this is the *Harry Potter* character Albus Dumbledore, whose name translates into 'white bumblebee'.

FOLIUM Any plant with *folium* in the title is bound to have something interesting about its leaves. Rosebay willowherb (*Epilobium angustifolium*) has narrow ones, yarrow (*Achillea millefolium*) has thousands of tiny ones and salsify (*Tragopogon porrifolius*) has leaves like a leek.

HALIO A Greek term relating to the sea or salt and often used to describe coastal plants like sea purslane (*Halimione portulacoides*), whose second name refers to a port or harbour. The English word halibios means the collective animals and plants that live in the ocean, compared to their populations on land.

LAMINARIA This Latin word for 'blades' is often used to describe different species of kelp, such as sugar kelp (*Laminaria saccharina*). Kelp species are known for having flat, blade-like fronds and the name for common kelp (*Laminaria digitata*) literally means 'blade fingers' – the Edward Scissorhands of the seaweed world.

OFFICINALIS A reference to a plant's use as a medicine or herbal remedy. It originates from the word *officina*, which was the name for the storeroom in a monastery where medicines were kept. One example of this is *Taraxacum officinale* or dandelion, which has historically been used to treat digestive problems and infections.

OLERACEA These plants can be used as a vegetable, grouped into the cultivar group *Brassica oleracea*. This includes cabbage, broccoli, kale, sprouts, savoy, cauliflower and collard greens.

PRATENSIS Signifying this plant grows in a meadow, such as goat's beard (*Tragopogon pratensis*) and cuckooflower (*Cardamine pratensis*).

SATIVUM Meaning 'sown' or 'cultivated' and originally used to refer to seed-grown domestic crops. While wild parsnip (*Pastinaca sativa*) and sweet chestnut (*Castanea sativa*) do pop up in the wild, they can also be planted and grown for more agricultural purposes.

SYLVESTRIS Used to describe plants that grow in woodlands and forests, such as the crab apple (*Malus sylvestris*) and the common mallow (*Malva sylvestris*). I think of Sylvanian Families, who were all woodland creatures and responsible for many of my happiest childhood memories.

VULGARIS Like the English word 'vulgar', this means a plant is considered common. It originates from the Latin *vulgus*, meaning multitude or masses and is used to refer to a plant that is easily found or rather plain. *Foeniculum vulgare* is the name for common fennel, a member of the carrot family.

WILDLIFE WATCH: WOODLAND

If you walk into a forest with your eyes closed, it is the aroma of growth and decay, fungus and soil that illuminates how much life exists around you. For a woodland is more than just trees in the ground and birds in the trees; it is a complex ecosystem connecting the softest worm buried deep within the earth, to the last molecule of oxygen released from a hazel leaf before the sun sets on another summer evening. Foraging is nature's great treasure hunt, and I sometimes catch myself ignoring the world around me to hunt down a particularly succulent plant for teatime. I try to remember the pleasing thing about plants is their immobility; while everything around us is fast-paced and hectic, that garlic mustard will still be waiting for you in a quiet corner of the woods, its fate sealed in a jar of fresh pesto. So, take the time to pause and watch the wildlife close by, for there is always something to see.

Tucked away beneath the leaf litter lies a microscopic world of beetles and spiders, their whole lives played out under the soles of our shoes. Did you know there are between three and eight million species of beetle on Earth? They

may seem insignificant, but they play a vital role in woodland ecosystems, feeding on debris from other animals and plants. Look out for the orange and black casings of sexton beetles, as well as the dor beetle, our largest dung beetle in Britain. The forest floor is also home to small rodents like wood mice, who store berries and seeds to keep them fed through the winter and the common toad, who lives away from water and likes to sleep in log piles. The rarest of all to be seen is the mole, one of our most common but secretive mammals who lives underground in a complex system of tunnels. He feeds on insects and centipedes and is even able to paralyse earthworms with his saliva.

A number of mammals patrol the woods, most of them familiar and Christmas card worthy. Rural foxes are much healthier than their urban cousins, their soft fur and chubby bellies warm against the night as they hunt for easy prey. At dusk, hedgehogs and badgers emerge from the gloom, crepuscular guardians of the forest. A third of our hedgehogs have disappeared over the last decade, primarily due to habitat loss and road accidents, but their numbers could see an increase if homeowners

carry out a few simple tasks to make their gardens hedgehog-friendly. Leave a CD-sized hole at the bottom of each fence panel to create a 'hedgehog highway', avoid using slug pellets and create a compost pile in the corner of your garden to provide a safe place for our hogs to hibernate.

Quiet foragers will be able to spot deer lurking between the trees; in Britain, we have sika, roe, red, muntjac, fallow and Chinese water deer, although no woodland is home to all six. Where I live in the South Downs, we watch fallow deer roam across the farmers' fields to take shelter in the forest nearby, where they eat grass, leaves, acorns, sweet chestnuts, bark, herbs and berries. For those further north, watch out for pine martens who have healthy populations in Scotland and Ireland, although they have also been recorded in Shropshire, the New Forest, the Lake District, Northumberland and the Yorkshire Moors.

Floating over the forest floor are the butterflies and woodland birds that bring a gentle buoyancy to the woods. Look out for orange tip butterflies drawn to cuckooflower and garlic mustard, as well as the purple hairstreak that lingers around oak trees. Other sylvan species include the peacock, silver-washed fritillary, speckled wood and white admiral, and hopping between them all are the birds of the forest. Brambling, chiffchaff and siskin feed either on insects or fresh seeds from alder, spruce, pine and birch, with the siskin being particularly fond of coniferous woodland; as are the goldcrest and firecrest, Britain's smallest (and cutest) birds that weigh the same as a 10p coin.

Finally, take a glance at the frothy, green canopy above and you'll find raptors gazing down at you with deep superiority. The magnificent goshawk hunts down mammals with crimson eyes and a distinctive white eyebrow; it weaves elegantly between trees, with its large wings, to catch prey. Although resident in Britain all year round, watch out for them in late winter and early spring, when they perform 'skydancing' displays to their peers. A walk in the dark will also expose you to the soft calls of tawny owls and, occasionally, the mating hoots of long-eared owls. For those with strong eyes, experience the rush of our woodland bats flying silently past in their pursuit of small insects.

INTRODUCING OUR COASTLINES

Did you know that nobody in Britain lives further than 80 miles from the seashore? Our vibrant and colourful coastlines have shaped a myriad of different habitats around the British Isles, including dramatic cliffs, sandy dunes and beaches, oozing estuaries, rocky shores and urban seaside towns. Each of these has played an important role in the evolution of our natural landscape, forming delicate ecosystems and contributing to the vibrant history of British culture.

The British Isles are formed of over 6,000 islands, and the coastline covers a total of 11,000 miles. The plants and animal species found within these areas are extensive, from the shallow waters that cover the continental shelves, through the rockpools and estuaries to the grasslands that thrive on salty soils. For most of us, a trip to the seaside might involve searching for crabs, eating chips and feeling the shingle beneath our sandals, but the coast is also a powerful tool with which our vulnerable isles protect themselves from the wrath of the ocean. The frictional drag across intertidal areas helps to absorb and dilute wave energy, so that seawater is less likely to encroach on our homes and towns.

A great way to explore the coastline is through beachcombing, an ancient hobby made famous by the novels of Herman Melville, who described how a group of 'beachcombers' living in the South Pacific, would search the shores for flotsam and jetsam to use or trade. Nowadays, it's a fun way to discover driftwood, seashells, man-made treasures and the occasional whalebone, although you may find a few pieces of litter too. Shockingly, more than eight million tonnes of plastic are dropped into our oceans every year, rather than being processed correctly with other waste; these

pieces of plastic find their way into our water, wildlife and seafood, damaging ecosystems and our own human health. Campaigns like the '2 Minute Beach Clean' and 'Plastic Oceans' are making significant progress with educating people on marine pollution, but the easiest way to help while you're foraging on British shores is to pop a few pieces of rubbish in your nearest bin and make our beaches even more beautiful.

For confident swimmers, the most invigorating way to experience the coastline is to brace yourself and take a dip. Wild swimming has seen a revival in recent years; when the tides are right and the water is calm, nothing feels more natural than to plunge into the brisk seas around Britain, surrounded by sunlight and the tickle of seaweed. Amy Liptrot's 2016 memoir *The Outrun* is a fantastic story of how wild swimming and engaging with the seas around Orkney helped restore the author to her former self and how wilderness itself can heal the mind and body.

Foragers can find plenty to nibble on the shores of the ocean. Plants like sea purslane, sea beet and common orache can be found throughout the year, while the exotic hottentot fig is juicy, invasive and in much need of harvesting to prevent it competing with native species. The bright orange berries of sea buckthorn are another useful discovery as, although the fruit is a little too tart to enjoy raw, they can be stewed into syrups or infused into vodka with a little thyme. Best of all, look out for vitamin-rich seaweeds floating through the water; prized and valued for their nutrients all over the world, plants like kelp, bladderwrack, carragheen and dulse can be used to thicken soups and sauces, or make delicious crisps with a few salt grains and chilli flakes.

HOTTENTOT FIG

CARPOBROTUS EDULIS June to September

Native to the hot shores of South Africa, the hottentot fig was introduced in the seventeenth century and is actually so invasive that it's an offence to knowingly plant them in the wild in Britain. The plant weaves itself into thick mats that form a carpet over warm coastal cliffs, preventing other species growing in the same spot and sometimes even altering the acidity of the soil. While this isn't great news for local wildlife, it does mean that the hottentot fig can be picked at leisure by seaside foragers. Flowers grow up to 10cm across with yellow, purple or bright pink petals and the fruits themselves are small and conical, although they do not much resemble the common fig. They are widely distributed along the coasts of southern Britain, but harder to find further north.

The figgy fruits are juicy and a little sour, as the temperatures in Britain are not quite high enough to allow the figs to ripen sweetly. They can be eaten raw, but if plenty are gathered they can be added to jams, chutneys and pickles. The fruits can also be stewed with sugar and spices to make a warm pudding, perfect with a dollop of thick cream.

SEA BEET

BETA VULGARIS SUBSP. MARITIMA March to October

Found along saltmarshes, shingle beaches and coastal footpaths, the sea beet is a halophyte, which means it has adapted to live in waters with high salinity. It is a sprawling but bushy plant with shiny leaves that can appear either oval-shaped or pointed, with reddish stems. It grows throughout Britain and Ireland and is thought to be the wild relative of common vegetables like beetroot and chard. The flowers are small and bright green, arranged in spiky clusters, but it's best to collect the leaves when the plant isn't flowering. While sea beet can grow in boisterous florets, try to avoid picking too much from the same spot.

Sea beet makes an excellent alternative to spinach, but avoid eating the tough stems as they can be unpleasant to chew. Try sautéing in butter as a side dish, or add chopped leaves to soups, mushroom lasagne, warm quiche, saag aloo, baked eggs, or stir into a frittata with fresh ricotta.

COMMON ORACHE

ATRIPLEX PATULA April to October

Also known as iron-root or spear saltbush, the common orache is found on waste ground, roadside verges and cultivated ground near coastlines. It is an archaeophyte plant, meaning it is not geographically native but was introduced in prehistoric times rather than through modern methods. The seeds have been found in the archaeological remains of Iron Age villages, combined with other cereal grains and the plant can now be found throughout southern Britain. The stems are minty white and the leaves are pointed and triangular with toothed edges. Flowers blossom in neutral tones, forming clusters in the leaf axils. Common orache can be mistaken for the inedible *Atriplex littoralis*, which is easily distinguished by its unpleasant taste and foul-smelling leaves.

Young leaves and shoots can be used in place of spinach, but they are a little bland and taste better when combined with spinach, chard or sorrel. Try sautéing all three to create a steaming bed for grilled monkfish, crumbled with a little feta.

SEA PURSLANE

HALIMIONE PORTULACOIDES All year

Often sprawled atop the walls of coastal footpaths, sea purslane tends to grow around saltmarshes, coastal dunes and pools and creek edges throughout the south and east of England (and sometimes even Scottish coasts in warm weather). Its ability to spread itself out means that it is often planted to stabilise sand dunes at risk of erosion. It's a lovely, fluffy plant, blossoming with greenish-yellow star-shaped flowers and thick, fleshy leaves and the entire thing is brimming with vitamins and minerals. Indeed, on some Caribbean islands it is used to treat wounds caused by venomous fish.

Due to their seaside surroundings, the leaves can be washed and eaten raw as they possess a crunchy, salty taste that makes them quite a tasty snack. Alternatively, they can be cooked like spinach, stir-fried with cashews, or served with any fish dish. In the Philippines they are called *dampalit* and are used with papaya and garlic to make sweet pickles called *atchara*.

MARSH SAMPHIRE

SALICORNIA EUROPAEA July to September

Found across the south and east coasts of England, marsh samphire makes its home in the gooiest of mudflats and saltmarshes and consequently bears a succulent, salty flavour that is nevertheless quite fresh. Also known as glasswort, the plant was historically burnt to make soda ash, a vital ingredient for the glass making process. The leaves are fused together to give the illusion of fleshy, leafless stems, so that popping up amidst a stark, marshy landscape they almost resemble saltwater cacti. Watch out for the closely related *Salicornia perennis* which, although edible, is considerably less delicious.

There are two options to harvest the plant. If there are plenty of specimens in the vicinity and they are not at risk of overpicking, the entire plant can be pulled up and washed thoroughly to remove tidal debris. Alternatively, use scissors to snip away the tops of the plant (a bit like asparagus stems) and leave the rest of the specimen to continue to grow and renew itself. Samphire can be eaten raw as a salty snack, or boil the trimmings in unsalted water for no more than 8–10 minutes. The soft flesh can then be removed from the stringy core and served as a side dish with butter. It also makes a fantastic accompaniment to any fish meal, particularly salmon.

BLACK MUSTARD

BRASSICA NIGRA March to September

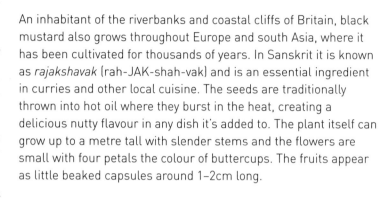

An inhabitant of the riverbanks and coastal cliffs of Britain, black mustard also grows throughout Europe and south Asia, where it has been cultivated for thousands of years. In Sanskrit it is known as *rajakshavak* (rah-JAK-shah-vak) and is an essential ingredient in curries and other local cuisine. The seeds are traditionally thrown into hot oil where they burst in the heat, creating a delicious nutty flavour in any dish it's added to. The plant itself can grow up to a metre tall with slender stems and the flowers are small with four petals the colour of buttercups. The fruits appear as little beaked capsules around 1–2cm long.

Like garlic mustard, the leaves can be used as a more vibrant alternative to spinach. Young leaves are particularly flavoursome and can also be added to salads, vegetable soups and quiches. The seeds can be eaten if you like a strong mustard flavour; if enough can be gathered, mix them with vinegar, white wine, salt and a little sugar to create a sharp and boisterous condiment.

WILD CABBAGE

BRASSICA OLERACEA All year

While this plant can be found across Britain, France, Spain and Italy, its intolerance of competitors and love of salty, calcareous soils means it is usually only found on chalk coastlines like those along the South Downs National Park. Popular with ancient Greeks and Romans, wild cabbage is the original ancestor of many familiar vegetables we pop in our shopping baskets each week, including cauliflower, cabbage, kale, broccoli and sprouts, all of which are rich in vitamins and carotenoids. The wild variety is a hairless plant with greyish-green leaves that are thick, long and fleshy. The flowers are bright yellow with petals that can grow up to an inch long.

Slightly more bitter than the domesticated variety, wild cabbage is never the less a fantastic addition to hot vegetables. Simply boil the young leaves and shoots before serving with spinach, asparagus or broccoli, along with a good blob of salted butter.

COMMON SCURVY-GRASS

COCHLEARIA OFFICINALIS April to October

Found in saltmarshes, coastal cliffs and saline springs, scurvy-grass grows along most British coastlines except the English Channel. The name scurvy-grass is a historical reference to its use by seafarers as a cure for scurvy before citrus fruits became more readily available to the public; the plant has a high vitamin content but its natural bitterness was usually masked with herbs and exotic spices. Modern wizarding fans might also recognise it as a key ingredient in the Befuddlement Draught, a potion studied by Harry Potter in *The Order of the Phoenix*. Leaves found at the base of the plant can be heart-shaped, kidney-shaped or rounded, with long stalks and small white petals arranged in loose spikes.

Although the leaves are a little bitter they can be effectively used like watercress or rocket, making a punchy addition to soups, salads, quiches, sandwiches and sauces.

LOVAGE

LIGUSTICUM SCOTICUM April to October

Lovage has carved a place for itself in medieval folklore, with a name that literally means 'love-ache' ('ache' being the medieval word for parsley). It was commonly thought to have aphrodisiacal qualities and King Charlemagne was so fond of the plant that he grew it in each of his many gardens. Today it is found on sea cliffs, rocky soils and on the coasts of Scotland and Northern Ireland, where it can grow up to 60cm tall and 1m wide. Stems are thick with large, toothed, diamond-shaped leaves and the flowers form yellow clusters like inside-out umbrellas. Wild lovage can be confused with the cultivated variety *Levisticum officinale*, a similar plant from southern Europe that is grown for its leaves, stems and roots, primarily for use in meat and vegetable extracts and herb liqueurs.

The leaves bear a strong aroma of celery and yeast and make a great addition to soups to enhance the flavour of other vegetables. They can also be used to wrap around red meat before roasting. As a herb, lovage partners well with oily fish and vegetable pasta and also makes a healthy tea full of B and C vitamins.

MILK THISTLE

SILYBUM MARIANUM April to June

Also known as blessed milk thistle, Marian thistle, Scotch thistle and Saint Mary's thistle, the common name is derived from the fact that the leaves are banded with speckles of white, like milk splashes. It is popular with herbalists as a medicinal treatment for liver problems and is usually found on roadsides, waste ground and sandy soils near coastlines across Britain, except in the very north of Scotland. Immediately recognisable for its lovely fuchsia flower head, the milk thistle has pinnate and prickly leaves, with yellowish-white spines that can be rather uncomfortable to touch. Look out for similar species *Cirsium arvense* (creeping thistle) and *Cirsium vulgare* (spear thistle) which, although different plants, can be used in the same way.

Before the flowers are able to develop, gather the young leaves and stems and remove any prickles. Boil these in salted water and sauté in butter to create a tasty vegetable dish. The roots can also be eaten raw or roasted with butter and the flower head itself can be eaten like a globe artichoke; try steaming it with a little garlic and lemon added to the water.

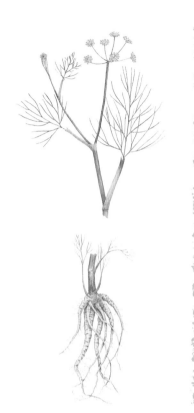

FENNEL

FOENICULUM VULGARE March to November

Wild fennel is most definitely a Marmite plant – you either love it or hate it. If you love star anise, liquorice root or cultivated fennel bulbs, then wild fennel is the plant for you. If, like me, you believe the taste of aniseed is a gift from Satan, you might not like the flavour. Either way, it's a fun plant to find on English and Welsh coastlines, where it tends to grow on sea cliffs and dry soils. Fennel has feathery green leaves that look a bit like dill, yellow flowers which are arranged in clusters of up to 30 and the fruits are oval and ridged. If you're not completely sure, crush the leaves between your fingers and you should catch the aroma of aniseed.

Throughout spring, the young leaves and stems taste great in soups, salads and light hot pots and make a particularly fine accompaniment to oily fish, chicken breasts and minced meat. The leaves can also be combined with cheese, garlic and breadcrumbs to make fennel cakes, or they can be added to couscous dishes with orange zest. In October the seeds can be gathered and used to flavour cakes and bread, but beware of their potent aroma!

SEA LETTUCE

ULVA LACTUCA All year

A rich source of iron, manganese, magnesium and potassium, sea lettuce is a popular food on the Okinawa islands just south of mainland Japan. It grows in saltwater areas with high nutrients, but this can mean that populations bloom and block out resources for other species in the area, so if you stumble upon a good haul, pick as much as you need. Most abundant in July and August, sea lettuce can be found at all tide levels across most British coastlines, particularly in rock pools, timberwork and any point where freshwater flows into the sea. The leaves are pale and watery green when they first appear, but grow to various sizes in a shade of darker green, gathered in bunches from one short stalk.

Fresh leaves can be gathered and added to salads, soups, noodle dishes and fish stews; they are particularly useful for wrapping around fresh fish before baking. Sea lettuce can also be dried out and ground into powder, which acts as a unique ingredient to enhance flavours and aromas in fish dishes, savoury biscuits and pizza toppings.

KELP or OARWEED
LAMINARIA DIGITATA All year

I love finding kelp; the Latin name *digitata* means fingers, because it looks like a big wobbly hand is waving at you underwater. Kelp has a lovely colouring of warm olives; the texture is thick and leathery with one wide blade tailoring off into strappy segments. It is usually found on low-tide rocky shores throughout Britain, sometimes forming 'kelp forests' on large tidal stones and, like marsh samphire, has historically been burnt to extract potash for the glass industry. The bottom of the plant bears a little foot that clasps tightly onto rocks, so it may be worth simply snipping a few of the blades off rather than trying to uproot the whole thing. Look out for the similar species *Laminaria hyperborea*, which has a rounder blade, a rougher surfaced stalk and grows at a greater depth. Although edible, *L. hyperborea* can harbour tiny marine creatures so it's best to forage for its smoother cousin, kelp.

Gather fresh blades in spring and early summer for the best flavour. In Japan, kelp is used as a thickening agent in soups and stocks, but it also makes a delicious condiment when dried and ground. Try sprinkling it on noodle soup with sustainable prawns and ginger.

SUGAR KELP

LAMINARIA SACCHARINA All year

Slightly sweeter than other varieties of kelp, sugar kelp is traditionally known as poor man's weatherglass; when humidity changes, the blades can become limp, dry or brittle: it was once used as a natural way to predict the weather. It can be found across British coastlines on rocky shores, sand flats and rock pools at middle shore depth and beyond. With its leathery fronds, iodine hue and crinkly edges, I imagine it to be like an old quill scribbling down the ocean's secrets. Like regular kelp, the stalk ends with a tiny foot that helps the plant grip onto rocks and resist the power of the waves.

Use this plant like you might use a bay leaf, adding to stews and casseroles to enhance the flavour. It can also be used raw in salads, added to soups as a thickener, or dried and ground as a tasty condiment.

BLADDERWRACK

FUCUS VESICULOSUS All year

Bladderwrack is one of the most common seaweeds you'll find sprawled along the middle shore and can often be spotted floating in the water at low tide, clinging to rocks, shells, timberwork and anything else it can attach itself to. It's the colour of dark olives and rather leathery, with pockets of air (bladders) swollen at the end of each branch and, like other seaweeds, secures itself onto rocks using a small rubbery foot. Of all the edible seaweeds in Britain, this is one of the richest in iodine and makes a tremendously healthy snack; in fact, it was the original source for the discovery of iodine in 1811.

Gather bladderwrack branches in spring and early summer for the best flavour. As it's so easy to find I use it to make seaweed crisps, a healthier alternative to the potato kind. Dry the branches off with kitchen towel and then lay them out flat on a baking tray. Sprinkle with sea salt, rosemary and chopped garlic and pop in the oven for a few minutes to bake, but watch carefully as they burn really quickly. It can also be added to soups and stews as a thickener, or dried and ground to be used as a condiment.

Seaweed
Frizzles

page 248

CARRAGHEEN OR IRISH MOSS

CHONDRUS CRISPUS All year

Usually found clinging to stones in rock pools, carragheen is a common seaweed across the middle and lower shores of the North Sea, English Channel and Atlantic Ocean. Aside from keen foragers, caragheen is also an important plant for amateur brewers in the UK; also known as Irish moss, it is a fantastic natural ingredient for beer, not adding much to the flavour but enabling the beer to clarify without the need to filter it. In the summer I brew nettle beer in my kitchen, adding caragheen to furnish the finished potion with a crisp, golden glow. For those who don't want to rely on mysterious brewery supply shops on eBay, head down to the shore and pluck your own ingredients fresh from the sea. Caragheen usually appears a dark red or minky pink colour, but in certain lights it may appear green; the frond is flat and fans out over rocks and stones in the shape of a tree. Look out for a similar plant known as batter frond (*Gigartina stellata*), darker in colour but with a similar tree-like shape, which is also edible and can be used in the same way as caragheen.

Gather in spring and summer for the best flavour and try making nettle beer - it's great fun and extremely easy! All you need is a bag of nettles, sugar, lemons, yeast, cream of tartar, caragheen and about two weeks of patience. Alternatively, use the gelatinous quality of caragheen to make a sweet, milky pudding like blancmange, tarted up with cinnamon and nutmeg.

PEPPER DULSE

OSMUNDEA PINNATIFIDA All year

Deliciously named the 'truffle of the sea', pepper dulse is famous for its powerful, punchy flavour and sanguine colouring, a ruby on the seabed that's hard to resist. The plant divides into progressively smaller branches, so the ends of each frond look like miniature tridents or giraffe horns. It tends to grow on middle and lower shores throughout Britain, especially on rock faces and hidden crevices; however, if found on exposed surfaces, you might discover the fronds have turned greenish.

Collect in spring and summer for the strongest flavour, although it will always be rather fiery. Sprinkle into stews, casseroles, soups and tagines, or try pan-frying mackerel fillets with a seasoning of pepper dulse, sea salt and chilli flakes. If you manage to find a good harvest, pick a little extra to dry and grind up into a perfect condiment for the kitchen cupboard.

DULSE

RHODYMENIA PALMATA All year

Historically, dulse has been eaten as an important source of dietary fibre throughout Norway, France, Scotland and Ireland for hundreds of years; in Iceland they eat it with butter and call it *söl*. While all seaweeds are considered super healthy, dulse is also thought to contain all trace elements needed in a balanced human diet and is a great source of protein for vegetarians. Found on most British coastlines, it usually grows on middle and lower shores on rocks and stones and even on the fattest stalks of other seaweeds. Dulse tends to grow in a palm shape (hence the scientific name) and the blades vary from burgundy to brick red and deep purple. It grips onto surfaces using a small, disc-shaped foot.

Dulse is best gathered from May to October and can be eaten fresh from the sea after a little rinse. Alternatively, lay the fronds out on warm rocks to dry in the sun to create a delicious, crispy snack. Add fresh pickings to soups, sandwiches and salads, or add to buttery mashed potatoes to make a traditional Irish 'champ'. My favourite seaweed dish is dulse nachos! Bake a few fronds in the oven and combine in a bowl with nachos, hot salsa, squashed avocado and Greek yoghurt. Sprinkle over a little cheese and enjoy a melted cosmos of seaside Mexicana.

LAVER

PORPHYRA UMBILICALIS All year

With young leaves of deep purplish-maroon, laver plants grow increasingly green with age and can reach a foot long. It's popular in eastern Asian cuisine, where it is known as *zicai* in China, *gim* in Korea and *nori* in Japan. In Britain it's found from higher shore to lower shore regions, clinging to rocks, boulders, timber structures and sand-covered stones on exposed beaches. It is extremely nutritious, particularly high in protein, iron and iodine levels, as well as vitamins A, B, C and D.

Laver weed is the core ingredient in *bara lafwr*, or laverbread, a traditional Welsh delicacy that is both squidgy and delicious. It is thought that, like local cheeses, each batch of bread is unique and will reveal different characteristics about the coastal landscape in which the laver was gathered; Richard Burton once declared laverbread to be 'the Welshman's caviar'. Boil the laver for six hours and then mix the resulting pulp with oatmeal. Squash the mixture into little cakes and fry in bacon fat or olive oil, before serving hot for breakfast with cockles or bacon for a traditional Welsh wake up.

SEA BUCKTHORN

HIPPOPHAE RHAMNOIDES September to January

The name *Hippophae* is a beautiful Greek word for 'glittering horse', as sea buckthorn leaves were the favourite food of the flying horse Pegasus and were often fed to racehorses to make them supple and speedy. While the leaves make a pleasant tea for humans, buckthorn's real glory lies within the bright, tangerine-coloured berries that decorate its prickly stems. They are incredibly rich in carotenoids, omega oils, antioxidants and vitamins C and E and have been used in traditional medicine for centuries throughout Tibet, China, Mongolia and Russia. They only grow in certain places in Britain, along coastlines with sandy soils and dunes where salt spray from the sea reduces competition from other plants. I tend to find mine in the West Country, but there are plenty of stocks in Scotland too. They are a favourite winter fruit for fieldfares.

The stems really are thorny, so be prepared when harvesting and take thick gloves and a bucket. Once enough berries have been gathered, they are best simmered down with sugar into a syrup. The raw berries are extremely sour but the sweeter syrup can be drizzled on granola for a vitamin boost. Raw berries can be slit and added to vodka for a sour spirit, or add a little syrup to champagne for a vibrant festive cocktail!

Wild Thyme & Sea Buckthorn Vodka

page 242

GODS AND MONSTERS

Of all the dark and mysterious places on earth, the sea is surely one of our most celebrated in mythology and folklore. Perhaps it is because there are so many pockets under the sea about which we still know so little. The deepest point in the seabed is the Challenger Deep section of the Mariana Trench; it measures almost 11,000m underneath the ocean's surface, and only four successful descents have ever been undertaken. Who knows what curious marine species dwell underwater, yet to be discovered and recorded in our history books? These mysteries have fuelled a large number of ancient myths across the globe, many of which date back thousands of years to the birth of 'civilised' man.

In Norse mythology, the sea giant Ægir is thought of as an ocean deity and is famous for hosting elaborate parties (my kind of guy). In the poem *Lokasenna*, Ægir throws a huge party for the gods and brews a giant cauldron full of delicious ale, which he serves to his guests. Perhaps it was made with bog myrtle, like the boozy drink brewed by the Norse warriors Úlfhéðnar? The Norse goddess Rán is also at one with the ocean and thought to be responsible for storms and those who die within them. Her nine daughters are known simply as the Waves, and she spends her immortal days beachcombing lost treasures at the bottom of the sea, gathering them together in the giant fishing net she wears around her waist.

The phrase 'Davey Jones' Locker' has been used for centuries as an idiom for the depths of the sea and the state of death among drowned sailors and shipwrecks. However, no one knows exactly how this phrase was born, nor when it was first used; the earliest written reference appears in Daniel Defoe's 1726 nautical tale *The Four Years Voyages of Capt. George Roberts*.

'Some of Loe's Company said, They would look out some things, and give me along with me when I was going away; but Ruffel told them, they should not, for he would toss them all into Davy Jones's Locker if they did.'

One theory suggests that Davey Jones' Locker originates from three words: 'Duppy', 'Jonah' and 'Locker'. Duppy is a Caribbean word for spirit or ghost; Jonah is a biblical figure who was thrown into the sea by his fellow sailors, only to be eaten by a giant fish; a locker is a nautical term for a storage space. Being thrown into Davey Jones' Locker, therefore, may loosely translate into 'being sent to a place of safekeeping, where Jonah's spirit was sent to.'

According to ancient Roman mythology, the goddess of saltwater was called Salacia, who ruled over the deepest parts of the ocean. Married to the mighty Neptune, she was at first so in awe of her noble suitor that she hid from him in the Atlantic Ocean. When Neptune could not find her, he sent a generous dolphin to bring her back and

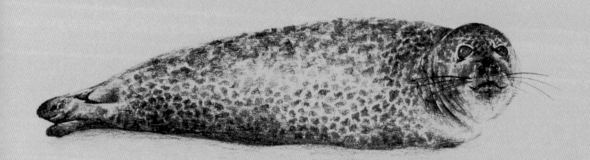

persuade her to share his watery throne. When she agreed, Neptune was so grateful that he awarded the dolphin a place in the heavens forever; he now forms the constellation Delphinus. While Neptune might be known for his stormy temper, Salacia represents the calmness of the sea; crowned with seaweed, she is carried forth in a pearl chariot drawn by dolphins and seahorses (a slight improvement on my Ford Focus).

One of our most famous creatures of the deep, the Leviathan is a huge sea monster that is often associated with chaos and the primordial world. First referenced in the Old Testament, Rabbi Johanan wrote that when he is hungry, the monster sends forth such heat that the waters around him boil. Although originally a biblical monster, the Leviathan has now become synonymous with any large sea creature feared by humans, such as the kraken, giant squid, hydra, behemoth and even the cyclops. In Alfred Lord Tennyson's sonnet 'The Kraken', he describes the murky dwelling of the creature:

> Below the thunders of the upper deep,
> Far, far beneath in the abysmal sea,
> His ancient, dreamless, uninvaded sleep
> The Kraken sleepeth: faintest sunlights flee
> About his shadowy sides; above him swell
> Huge sponges of millennial growth and height;
> And far away into the sickly light,
> From many a wondrous grot and secret cell

> Unnumbered and enormous polypi
> Winnow with giant arms the slumbering green.
> There hath he lain for ages, and will lie
> Battening upon huge sea worms in his sleep,
> Until the latter fire shall heat the deep;
> Then once by man and angels to be seen,
> In roaring he shall rise and on the surface die.

In Inuit mythology, Sedna is the goddess of the sea and all marine animals and also rules over the Inuit underworld known as Adlivun. There are numerous versions of the Sedna legend, but my favourite is this one: Sedna is a beautiful woman who rejects proposals of marriage from every hunter in her village. One day, a new hunter appears, and her father agrees to sell his daughter to him for a few fish (cheers, Dad). Having given Sedna a sleeping potion, he hands her over to the hunter who carries her to a large nest on a cliff, revealing his true form as a great bird-spirit in the shape of a fulmar. Overcome by guilt, her father returns to rescue her in a kayak, but when her captor discovers his loss, he becomes enraged and sends a storm to kill them both. Her father decides to throw Sedna overboard to appease the bird-spirit (much obliged, Father), but she clings to the kayak with all her might. Her father then chops off three of her fingers, which become three different species of seal, before striking her on the head (so much love) and sending her to the depths of the ocean, where she resides forever with the animals of the sea.

WILDLIFE WATCH: COAST

Britain has always been a nation of bird lovers, and our coastline is one of the most fantastic places to kick back with a pair of binoculars and a hot cup of tea to watch the organised chaos of our coastal birds. 'Seagulls' are common and familiar to most who have cherished a seaside portion of salty chips, only to have one snatched away by an opportunistic individual. The word 'seagull', however, is almost blasphemous to the birdwatching community as the word does not relate to a single species; it has become an umbrella term for a number of different species of gull, all of which have long wings, strong legs and can swim buoyantly. These include the herring gull, black-headed gull, kittiwake, lesser black-backed gull and the paler iceland gull.

With such a range of different coastal habitats around the country, there are some truly exciting bird species to discover if you know where to look. From March to August, breeding colonies of puffins are common in Scotland, Wales and Cornwall, although they can also be found around the north of England on sites like Bempton Cliffs in the East Riding of Yorkshire. With its tubby shape and beautiful, bright beak, the puffin is also known as a 'sea parrot' and eats hake, herring and sandeels. Elsewhere, look out for oystercatchers feeding on cocklebeds and large gannets who arrive just after Christmas and stay until harvest time. Guillemots and razorbills are always wonderful to watch and, on muddy shores, watch out for wading birds like redshanks, dunlins, curlews, sanderlings and godwits, who use their differently sized beaks to share worms, shellfish and shrimps that live at varying depths within the sand.

The coast doesn't just belong to the birds (although they probably think it does). It's also a great place to look out for marine mammals like the harbour porpoise, otters and seals. We have two different

species of seal in Britain - the grey seal and the common seal. Grey seals are much larger and are famous for their long, sloping noses. They spend most of their time at sea or on rocky shores with their white, fluffy pups appearing towards the end of autumn, where they remain on land until they have moulted and can hunt for themselves. The smaller common seal has a more dog-like face and is usually found on sheltered shores and estuaries where it feeds on fish, squids, whelks, crabs and mussels. They will often hold their head and tail in the air at the same time, like a cute banana.

One of the most exciting species to watch from the shoreline is the bottle-nosed dolphin, a mammal many Britons don't tend to associate with our waters. The best places to spot them include Cardigan Bay in Wales and the coasts of Cornwall, Dorset and Devon. Usually found in pods of 15 members or so, they are sociable, acrobatic and full of fun, often leaping from the water and performing somersaults between their searches for fresh fish. Amazingly, an individual bottle-nosed dolphin can live for up to 50 years in the wild. If you're lucky, you may even spot other cetaceans in the water, particularly in Scotland where there are regular sightings of orcas, humpback whales, minke whales and even basking sharks.

While the skies and seas are full of extraordinary wildlife, don't forget to look down to discover a microscopic world beneath your feet. Rockpooling is an excellent way to fill a balmy afternoon by the sea, where you might find crabs, shrimps, starfish, whelk, razor shells, prawns, mussels and barnacles in the shallow waters. I also love finding shells and pebbles that have been smoothed by the saltwater; I usually pop a few in my pocket and use them for crafts later on. Always be sure to remember to check the tide times before you set out, or you may get a little stuck!

INTRODUCING HEATHLAND

To many of us, heathland is simply a beautiful and evocative place in which to walk our dog, pull up Christmas trees or listen to nightjars. The truth is that while in Britain we are fortunate enough to have 58,000 hectares of heathland, globally it is a rarer habitat than rainforest. Since 1800 we have lost an enormous portion of what we once had, with only 16 per cent left of the heathland that once existed here; poetry lovers may be familiar with the issues surrounding this habitat through the work of John Clare, a nineteenth-century poet from Northamptonshire.

Clare grew up within the whirlwind of the Industrial Revolution. As factory work became mechanised and the cities grew, the countryside was ploughed up, fens drained, trees uprooted, and heathland (also known as common land) was enclosed. What had once been, literally, common land for communities to graze their livestock and collect firewood, became included in one larger plot of land owned by whoever could afford to buy it. This landlord then controlled how the land was used and although yields and profits increased, many people felt it signalled the end of the communal countryside. Tenants were no longer able to graze upon the land unless permission was granted and many poorer people were forced to leave the rural areas for factory work in the cities nearby.

The effect on John Clare's landscape and particularly the common heathland, was so intense that he produced reams of poetry on the disruption of the countryside, nature and the alienation of the self, much of which was triggered by the Enclosure Acts in the latter half of the nineteenth century. In the extract below, from his poem *The Mores*, he remembers what life on the heath was like before enclosure:

> ...The sheep and cows were free to range as then
> Where change might prompt nor felt the bonds of men
> Cows went and came, with evening morn and night,
> To the wild pasture as their common right
> And sheep, unfolded with the rising sun
> Heard the swains shout and felt their freedom won
> Tracked the red fallow field and heath and plain
> Then met the brook and drank and roamed again
> The brook that dribbled on as clear as glass
> Beneath the roots they hid among the grass
> While the glad shepherd traced their tracks along
> Free as the lark and happy as her song...

In many ways, we seem to have come full circle in our relationship with the landscape. A good portion of the heathland once 'owned' by nineteenth-century landowners has now been handed back to the public in the form of National Trust reserves, like the Devil's Punchbowl in Surrey, or nature reserves like the Wildlife Trusts' Iping Common in Sussex. These are glorious places to wander and breathe in the sweet aroma of heather and should continue to be protected for years to come. While the historical loss of British heathland is a sad statistic, much of what is left is now being nurtured and maintained by conservationists.

Due to the tiddly size of the British Isles, few of us have to travel far to find a wild patch of heathland. It grows on acidic, dry sandy or wet peaty soils and can be recognised by the presence of numerous dwarf-shrubs, including heather, gorse, bilberry, cowberry and crowberry. As a habitat, it is home to a number of specialised plants and animals, one of the most important reasons to protect and nurture it; these include reptiles, birds, invertebrates and plants. One land management tool, that may surprise foragers, is the use of fire to burn sections of heathland to remove old growth and allow fresh

plants to thrive. It can appear counterproductive and slightly hooligan-esque from afar, but it's a method that has been used for hundreds of years to promote a fresh flush of plant growth for livestock to graze on. Species of heather are particularly beneficial to burn, as their seeds are adapted to germinate at high temperatures.

The heath is a fantastic location to forage for some truly marvellous plants. Throughout the year grows the familiar common gorse, its lemon-yellow blossom dizzy with the scent of coconut protected deep behind rows of grizzly thorns. Some berries can be harvested on heathland, including juniper for gin, bilberries for muffins and cranberries for breakfast; the rowan tree is another favourite, but those tangerine berries will have to be argued over with the many heathland birds that also enjoy their flavour. But it's the heather that looks the most spectacular on a balmy summer afternoon; long stems swathed across the landscape in a thousand shades of pink, a forager for heather will also encounter some of our most beautiful butterflies and bumblebees as they too seek the same sweet nectar.

COMMON GORSE

ULEX EUROPAEUS January to June

A familiar flowering plant across most British heathlands, the gorse bush is both beautiful and vicious. Sprinkled with yellow flowers, the thickets are also covered in small, hard spines that make foraging incredibly difficult, although still worth it. Like many gorse species across the world, common gorse is a fire-climax plant, which means it catches fire easily but regrows with renewed health and vigour afterwards. A burning gorse plant generates so much heat that it was often used in medieval bread ovens to fuel a tasty fire. The seeds themselves are adapted to germinate after being scorched and most heathland nature reserves use controlled burning as a method of maintaining vegetation and promoting new growth. The shrub itself is a large, evergreen species and can flower throughout the year, blossoming most frequently in spring.

The petals have a delicious, coconutty aroma that is definitely worth capturing if you have the patience. Gloves aren't much use at this point as the flowers are so small you'll need full use of your hands to reach between the thorns. Once enough petals have been gathered, use them to make a delicate panna cotta, sweet cakes or my gorse honey mead with a chilli kick.

Gorse Kick Mead
page 238

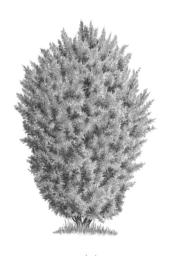

JUNIPER

JUNIPERUS COMMUNIS September to February

Most will know juniper as the blessed tree that brings the gift of gin, as the berries are used as a prime flavouring for the spirit, along with other delicious botanicals. The tree itself is small and bushy, with reddish bark and needle-like leaves; these are stiff and bluish-green in colour, with a white band running through the middle. Like sloe berries, juniper fruits ripen from green to indigo, but unlike sloes, the juniper berry takes two or three years to develop fully. They grow throughout Britain on chalky soils and shallow acid peat, usually found in downland, heath, moors and woodlands near pine and birch. Foragers will find themselves in the company of a variety of birds; firecrests and goldcrests take cover in the tree's thick foliage, while the berries provide food for the fieldfare, ring ouzel, song thrush and mistle thrush. As juniper populations are struggling at the moment, it's best to leave plenty of berries for these birds who will help spread seeds and create precious gin for the future. In Scandinavia, juniper wood is also used to make containers for butter and cheese, due to its pleasant aroma and strength.

Try to gather the fruits before they are fully ripe. They can be used in marinades and dry rubs for meat, particularly venison, beef and lamb, or you can make a pleasant herbal tea. Alternatively, whizz them up for pâté with duck or mushrooms, or add them to sweet desserts with apples and pears.

BILBERRY

VACCINIUM MYRTILLUS July to September

The bilberry fruit can often be mistaken for the North American blueberry, a much more familiar berry that tends to fill our granola bowls and smoothies. In America, bilberries are affectionately called huckleberries; their tiny size means they are often used to refer to something small. Usually found on elevated heaths, moors and woods on acidic soils, they are a rare find in Britain but very popular in Scandinavia as a source of vitamin C. The bilberry shrub is small and evergreen with bright oval leaves and bulbous flowers of greenish-pink, while the berries are tiny blue-black globules with a whitish bloom of natural yeast.

Bilberries are slightly tarter than their New World cousins, but they are still sweet and delicious raw, particularly scattered over porridge, yoghurt and fruit salads. Embrace American cuisine with a range of bilberry pies, muffins and cookies, or simmer the fruits down to a compote and drizzle over desserts. They also make a fantastic summer pudding combined with raspberries, blackberries and redcurrants.

CRANBERRY

VACCINIUM OXYCOCCUS August to October

A staple ingredient of Christmas cuisine, the cranberry was so named by early European settlers in America, who thought the flowers looked like the unfolding head and beak of a crane. Native American communities were the first to use the cranberry in cooking, medicine and cloth dying and some historians believe the Algonquian people of the Atlantic coast first introduced the berries to hungry colonists in Massachusetts, who then used them in traditional Thanksgiving feasts. In Britain, the cranberry shrub is found in wet heaths and peat bogs, although it is uncommon in England, Wales and Ireland. The shrub itself is evergreen with small, spreading leaves up to 10mm long; its 'crane-like' flowers are pinkish-red with a crimson, bulbous berry up to 6mm wide.

Cranberries are notoriously tart if eaten raw, but when cooked they make an excellent ingredient for jams and jellies to accompany roast meat. Alternatively, sprinkle over granola for a sharp but healthy vitamin boost, or add whole to pâtés and stodgy stuffings in winter. They also liven up homemade breads and cakes – try my cranberry and hazelnut loaf with lots of butter.

Hazelnut
& Cranberry
Loaf
page 230

HEATHER

CALLUNA VULGARIS July to September

There's nothing more delightful than wandering through an acre of heather on a warm afternoon in August. Each flower marks the discovery of a delicate new shade of pink and the air quivers with fat bees bumping from petal to petal in search of nectar. The most dominant species of any British heathland, heather is common throughout the country and grows in small, evergreen shrubs with arrow-shaped fronds. It has traditionally been utilised as a food source for grazing livestock, such as sheep and wild deer. If you can find a pot in your local farm shop, heather honey is full of intense flavours from the local flora, sprucing up platters of hot toast and tea.

Heather was once used as an alternative to hops in beer making and home brewers may like to try concocting their own ales and wines. The flowers are wonderfully sweet and can be dried and infused with bramble leaves and thyme to make a delicious herbal tea.

ROSEBAY WILLOWHERB

EPILOBIUM ANGUSTIFOLIUM April to June

Known as 'bombweed' in the south of England, willowherb is known for its tolerance and adaptability to waste ground and has historically been used to recolonise bomb craters, oil spills and other disturbed sites. In wartime Britain, many woodlands were burnt and cleared to make way for human expansion and military activity, resulting in a huge surge in rosebay willowherb and the survival of a healthy population today. Growing together in large clusters, it is instantly recognisable for its long, pointed leaves and bright pink flowers that reach high up into the sky, a delectable jungle for local pollinators. Found in heathland, woodland, mountains and waste ground, it is also a great plant to forage in cities and other urban areas.

Young shoots of willowherb can be steamed with butter for an asparagus-like side dish. The leaves can be added to salads or cooked like spinach and the roots can be unearthed in late autumn to be roasted with parsnips, carrots and garlic cloves. In Russia, willowherb leaves were traditionally used to make *Koporye* (koh-POR-yee) tea, a pleasantly tart drink named after a village in Leningrad Oblast where the plant was originally harvested.

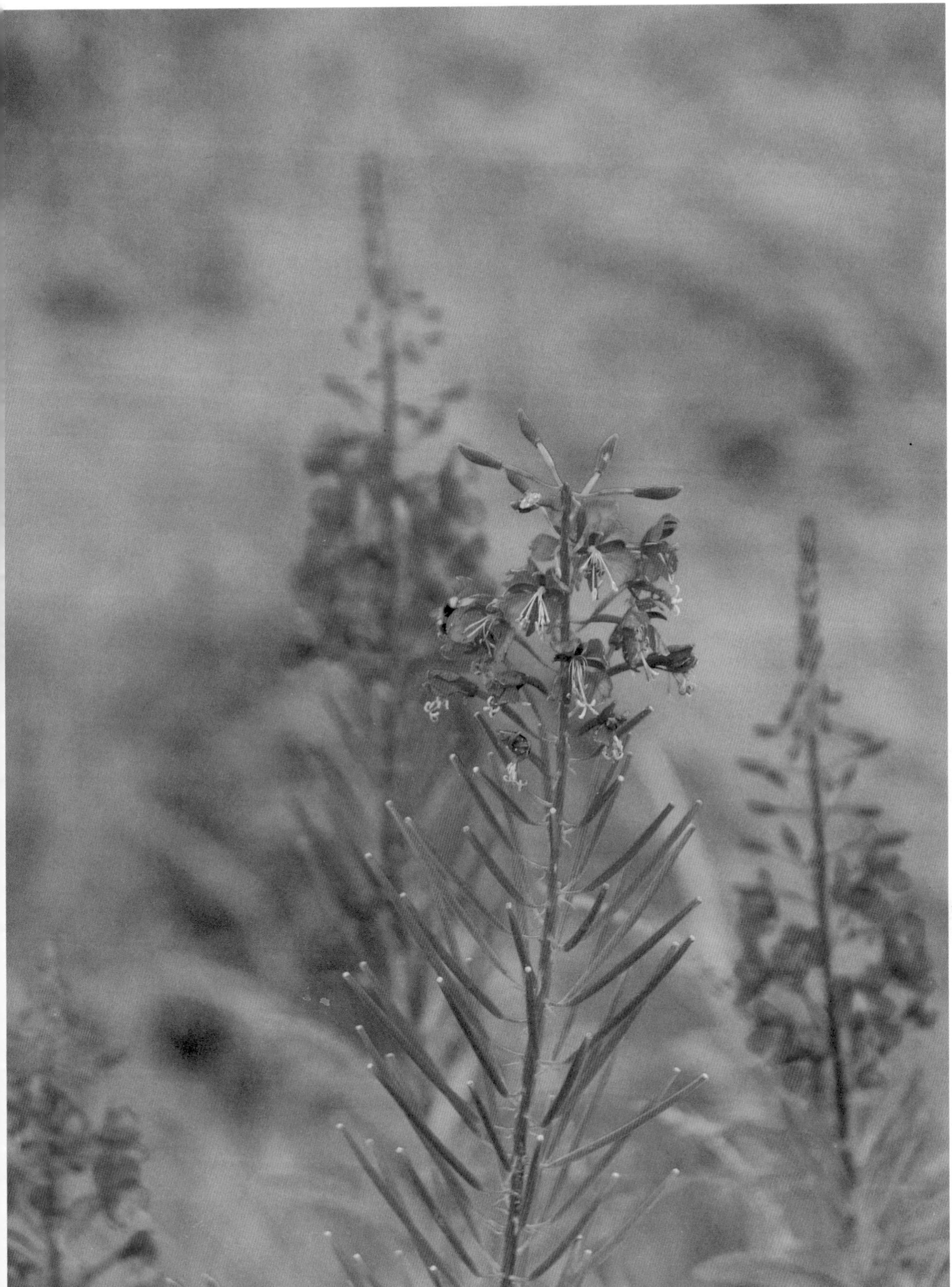

WILD THYME

THYMUS SERPYLLUM All year

Wild Thyme is a common plant throughout Britain, but it tends to grow only on heathland, dry grasses and sandy soils where it attracts bees and common blue butterflies. Like domesticated thyme grown in pots on kitchen windowsills, the fronds of wild thyme form a dense mat of aromatic leaves, tipped with pink, purple and white flowers arranged in thick clusters. Growing a mere 10cm off the ground, the herb has historically been used to raise the spirits with its Mediterranean aroma and was a favourite remedy for Roman citizens struck with melancholia.

Wild thyme can be used in exactly the same way as its domesticated cousin, but bear in mind the former has a weaker flavour and should be used in greater quantities. Dry a few sprigs and grind them up for an essential addition to the kitchen cupboard, or use them fresh in stuffings, soups and poultry dishes. Try adding a few leaves to a thick, autumn risotto with mascarpone, butternut squash and chestnuts, or combine with lemons and limes to make a warm lemon drizzle cake with a fragrant twist.

BOG MYRTLE

MYRICA GALE May to October

While the sweet scent of bog myrtle leaves has rendered it a traditional plant in royal wedding bouquets, it was also once thought to hold magical powers; historians believe a group of Norse warriors known as the Úlfhéðnar (ulf-hied-nirh) brewed the leaves into a boozy drink to cast themselves into a trance-like rage, readying themselves for bloody battle. Today, it is a fairly peaceful plant growing locally throughout Britain, except in the southeast, on moors and heathland with more acidic soils. The fragrant leaves are long and oval-shaped, but red (female) and orange (male) catkins grow before the leaves and contain small, purplish seeds.

Like many plants, the leaves were once used for flavouring beer before hops became popular in Britain. Home brewers can give this a go and they can also be used as a botanical to flavour homemade spirits like gin. Alternatively, the leaves and berries can be dried and added to autumn stews, or chopped and combined with butter and wild marjoram to make a delicious coating for roast chicken.

CHAMOMILE
CHAMAEMELUM NOBILE June to July

Known historically for its anti-inflammatory properties, the chamomile flower was once fairly common in Britain, but has now been pushed back to only a few areas in southern England. The name stems from the Greek for 'earth apple', as the leaves release the scent of fresh apple when crushed, but visually the plant will often be mistaken for a wild daisy at first glance. With creeping, feathery leaves and flowers up to 2.5cm wide, it can be distinguished from other plants by the lack of soft down on the underside of its leaves. Look for it on heaths and pastures around the New Forest where it blossoms in the first flush of summer.

The best use for chamomile is to pick a few heads, dry them at home and infuse them in hot water for a delicate tea. Chamomile is classed as vulnerable in Britain so it's important not to pick too many; fortunately you will only need a couple of heads to make an infusion.

BITTER VETCH

LATHYRUS MONTANUS September to December

Found on heaths, scrub, hedges and woodland, bitter vetch is common throughout Britain except on the Saxon plains of East Anglia. It was historically grown by Highland communities until the eighteenth century, when potatoes became a core part of their diet and replaced the smaller tubers of bitter vetch. Medicinally, they are also thought to have appetite-suppressing properties that prevent the miserable pangs of hunger and thirst. Above ground they bear reddish-blue flowers arranged in clusters of two to six, with winged stems and leaves divided into linear leaflets.

From September to Christmas, small tubers can be dug out of the ground where there is an abundance of plants. Although they can be eaten raw, they are best steamed, boiled or roasted to release a sweet flavour similar to chestnuts. Try boiling, chopping and sautéing in butter with garlic for an excellent side dish.

ROWAN or MOUNTAIN ASH

SORBUS AUCUPARIA August to November

With its blood-orange berries and a habit of towering over the most desolate of heathlands, it is no mystery that the rowan tree has carved itself into the darkest corners of British folklore. Long associated with magic and witchcraft, its old Celtic name was *fid na ndruad* (the wizards' tree); its silver-grey bark was thought to ward off evil powers from other worlds and was even used to stir milk to prevent curdling. While we may not worry too much about witchcraft today, the rowan tree still makes a fantastic species to forage and autumn visitors may benefit from spotting the blackbird, mistle thrush, redstart, redwing, song thrush, fieldfare and waxwing all fattening up on berries for the winter. The fruits grow from bright yellow to tangerine, finally ballooning into a scarlet berry brimming with vitamin C.

Try to resist picking the berries until they are fully ripe. While they can be eaten raw, they are extremely sour and are best simmered down into syrups, jams and jellies. Rowan jelly makes a fantastic accompaniment to cheeseboards and hot meat, but remember to add cooking apples to ensure pectin levels are high enough to set.

Hedgerow
Jelly
page 216

SECRETS OF THE HEATH

With such a moody and evocative terrain, it's no wonder the heather moors of Britain have been used as iconic backdrops in many folk stories and literary classics. Dartmoor National Park in Devon is the natural home to feral ponies, forests, rivers and huge tors, but nestled between are also Neolithic tombs, stone circles, abandoned medieval dwellings and a prison dating back to the slave trade. It is also the setting for Arthur Conan Doyle's *The Hound of the Baskervilles*, where Sherlock Holmes must solve the riddle of a fearsome hound that is terrifying people to death. A number of other ghost stories have all grown in Dartmoor, from headless riders and ghost brides to haunted houses and eerie spots where the gallows once stood. In the town of Ashburton in southern Dartmoor, there is said to live an evil sprite called Cutty Dyer who waylays drunkards and throws them in the river, so be sure to lay off the sloe gin when wandering dark pathways...

Egdon Heath is a fictitious area of Thomas Hardy's Wessex, an area in south-west England in which he set most of his novels, including *Jude the Obscure*, *Tess of the D'Urbervilles* and *Far from the Madding Crowd*. Most of Hardy's fiction takes place in rural landscapes tinted with nostalgia and Egdon is inhabited by the 'commoners' who cut the gorse (known as furze) that grows there. In *The Mayor of Casterbridge*, Hardy describes the ancient landscape in which his tale is set:

> He had left the Melchester coachroad at Weatherbury by a forking highway which skirted the north of Egdon Heath. Into this road they directed the horse's head, and soon were bowling across that ancient country whose surface never had been stirred to a finger's depth, save by the scratching of rabbits, since brushed by the feet of the earliest tribes.

Fifty years later, Daphne du Maurier published her famous novel *Jamaica Inn*, a gloomy tale of smugglers and murder set in the desolate Bodmin Moor in northeast Cornwall. It was inspired by a real visit to Jamaica Inn, a tavern built in 1750 that was used as a coaching inn and smugglers' checkpoint. Between 1984 and 2003, the same inn was used to house a large collection of taxidermy animals in bizarre dioramas, known as 'Mr Potter's Museum of Curiosities' and included a schoolroom populated by baby squirrels and kittens playing croquet. Sounds creepy? It was. I visited Jamaica Inn when I was very small and the exhibition was still there. My dad tried to assure me that all the animals had died of natural causes; it haunts me to this day.

One of the most famous meetings upon the heath is that of the witches, the Wëird Sisters, in Shakespeare's Scottish tragedy Macbeth. In their own odd way they were foragers too, although nowadays the wild ingredients taken from the heath and plopped in their cauldron would probably get them in trouble with various animal rights' groups:

> Double, double, toil and trouble,
> Fire burn and cauldron bubble.
> Fillet of a fenny snake
> In the cauldron boil and bake;
> Eye of newt, and toe of frog,
> Wool of bat, and tongue of dog;
> Adder's fork and blind-worm's sting,
> Lizard's leg, and howlet's wing:
> For a charm of powerful trouble,
> Like a hell-broth, boil and bubble.

I'm not sure how much of a naturalist Will Shakespeare was, but these ingredients are surprisingly accurate for a heathland habitat, which would include snakes, newts, frogs, bats, adders, slow worms (blind-worms), lizards and owls (howlets). Being vegetarian, however, I would be interested in a plant-based version of this intriguing dish; hopefully, the Sisters will branch out.

Perhaps the most famous heathland tales of all are those of the Brontë sisters, set against the desolate landscape of the Yorkshire Moors and full of dark twists and doomed romances that many believe capture the hostile beauty of the heath. Authors of classic novels Wuthering Heights, Jane Eyre and The Tenant of Wildfell Hall, Emily, Charlotte and Anne Brontë captured the soul of the moorland in the evocative descriptions within which their stories were set. In Wuthering Heights, Catherine Earnshaw lies dying in bed, but longs to be outside in nature, where she feels she belongs:

> Oh, I'm burning! I wish I were out of doors – I wish
> I were a girl again, half savage and hardy, and free ...
> and laughing at injuries, not maddening under
> them! Why am I so changed? Why does my blood
> rush into a hell of tumult at a few words? I'm sure
> I should be myself were I once among the heather
> on those hills ... Open the window again wide,
> fasten it open!

When she is finally laid to rest, she is not buried in a grave, but on a green slope in the corner of the churchyard, 'where the wall is so low that heath and bilberry plants have climbed over it from the moor.'

WILDLIFE WATCH: HEATHLAND

The unique structure of heathland habitat means the wildlife found there forms a complex but beautiful ecosystem of its own; this is one of the main reasons heathland is so important to manage and protect. With stout carpets of heather in pink, coral, salmon, rose and lilac, the moors are a perfect spot to look for pollinators. A number of rare bumblebees can be found on lowland heathland, including the tormentil mining bee, potter flower-bee, brown-banded carder bee and long-horned bee, plus several uncommon butterflies like the high brown fritillary, pearl-bordered fritillary, grayling and silver-studded blue. Bees and butterflies love the sweet nectar of heather flowers and will wander lazily across the heaths on summer mornings in search of breakfast.

The stoat is my favourite heathland mammal, easy to differentiate from weasels as it is much larger and has a long tail with black tip (plus a stoat is stoatally different, and a weasel is weasily recognised). With chestnut fur and a creamy white belly and throat, they have a distinctively arched shape when running around, much like a squirrel. Preying on smaller rodents and rabbits, they mate in the summer but withhold pregnancy until the

following spring, when they produce one litter of tiny kits. They are also known as ermine, the name given to them in winter when their coats will often turn a bright, snowflake white.

Watch out for the quiet rustle of foliage as an adder slithers through the grass. Adders can have a poor reputation as they are the only venomous snake in Britain, but they are thought to be very gentle and calm, only attacking a dog or human if they are trampled on or heavily disturbed. Foragers who stumble upon a log pile on a sunny August afternoon should have a careful peek within, as adders love basking in the sun and will often lie completely still, perfectly camouflaged against the bark and bracken. Lizards will follow suit as, being cold-blooded creatures, they need warm sunbeams to raise their body temperature and kickstart their daily activities.

Bird lovers should keep an eye out for skylarks, Dartford warblers and stonechats, who eat a variety of seeds, insects and fruit that grow on the heath. Small and brown with a funky tuft at the back of their heads, skylarks are famed for their dramatic display flights high up in the air, as celebrated in Shelley's 1820 poem *To a Skylark*:

Higher still and higher
From the earth thou springest
Like a cloud of fire;
The blue deep thou wingest,
And singing still dost soar, and soaring ever singest.

The stonechat is instantly recognised for its chirping song, likened to two pebbles being tapped together; their vibrant rust-coloured chests are easy to spot and to watch a pair hopping about among the gorse provides endless entertainment. Dartford warblers are limited to the south of England but are well worth a visit to listen to their gossiping warble.

On dry days, get down on your hands and knees and find yourself absorbed in the comings and goings of heathland bug life. The large minotaur beetle is a fantastic one to spot, a glossy, black dung beetle with enormous horns (like their titular Greek monster); look for them near rabbit droppings in the evenings. When dusk has properly settled, those with keen eyes may discover one of our most magical beetles, particularly in the south of England, lowland Scotland and Wales. The female glow-worm emits a bright green-orange light from their bottom, climbing up plant stems to seduce males and secure a mate. They are extremely small, but the light of a glow-worm is unmistakable and a mesmerising treat on a dark summer night; look out for them around June and July.

When summer nights close in between June and August, make time to embark on a nocturnal ramble to listen to the nightjar and its eerie, churring song. A cross between a cuckoo and a kestrel, nightjars are tough to spot in the daytime, as they nest on the ground and their feathers are the colour of bark. At night, use their churring call to get close to their secret location and wait. When the song stops, the nightjar could be about to clap its wings and lift off, and you might be able to spot its ghostly silhouette against the moonlight. Their eerie reputation originates so far back that their Latin scientific name *Caprimulgus europaeus* refers to an old superstition that they entered farmsteads at night and stole milk straight from the goat's udder. Once heard, the churr of the nightjar cannot be forgotten; I make a special pilgrimage every summer to hear it drifting across the darkened landscape.

INTRODUCING MEADOWS

Traditional wildflower meadows are an essential part of our rural landscape. An acre of bright flowers rippling on a summer morning will be purring with bees and butterflies, forming a remarkable ecosystem that so much of our food production relies upon. Before the Second World War, lowland meadows were a familiar habitat across most of the country, but due to a change in farming practices like intensive ploughing, drainage, fertiliser and herbicide application, we have lost over 95 per cent of our meadows in the last few decades alone. That's because lowland meadows are managed by humans, despite their feral appearance; without due attention, their delicate balance of flowers and plants can become overrun by competitive species like brambles and many vulnerable flowers can be shaded out by tougher grasses.

A healthy meadow will frequently hold up to 30 different grass species and a hundred or more wildflowers, including pepper saxifrage, cuckooflower, poppy, rosebay willowherb, yellow iris, agrimony, celandine, tansy, primrose and purple loosestrife. These attract a range of different pollinators, like bumblebees and the meadow brown and marbled white butterflies. In turn, these attract rare horseshoe bats and declining farmland birds like the skylark and corncrake, whose Latin name *Crex crex* is a perfect mimic of its rasping call. The corncrake's habitat has become so diminished that it is now extinct in lowland Britain, except for the Outer Hebrides.

More recently, conservation groups have been working with farmers to help reduce their impact on wildlife and start farming alongside nature, rather than against it. One lovely example of this is through conservation grazing, a scheme that uses livestock to graze habitats like meadows and grassland to create organic mosaics of different grass lengths and microhabitats. When humans started farming the land at the end of the Stone Age, they cleared large areas of trees to form open spaces, which in turn helped to shape many of our

most valuable habitats for wildlife. To ensure these species can continue to thrive, a little management must be put into practice to maintain these areas and help to nurture healthy populations of flora and fauna.

The majority of livestock used for conservation grazing are cattle, sheep and ponies, with native breeds often selected for their hardiness amidst the British weather. As a general rule, grazing animals will naturally choose to eat the more dominant plant species, which allows the less competitive ones to access a little more sunlight and soil nutrients and consequently become more established. Without wheels or clunky metal parts, a grazing animal is also able to reach areas that machinery can't, while also doing less damage, just as heavy horses are sometimes used to remove fallen trees from forests without uprooting other trees on the way. The dung of livestock is also crucial to creating healthy ecosystems, as the invertebrates that feed on their nutrients will in turn feed rodents, small mammals, birds, bats and badgers.

It's easy to lend a helping hand to our wildflower meadows. Ask your local Wildlife Trust if you're interested in joining a working conservation group on the ground, or simply become a member to help fund wildflower projects. There are also charities that provide free wildflower seeds and planting advice to help grow more species across the country, so try to plant a few species in your local area with friends or family. You could also look out for wildlife-friendly farms that specialise in traditional management and support them by buying their produce and spreading the word.

Healthy meadows are a wonderful place to forage fresh plants for light summer cuisine. Wait for the aroma of wild rose and guelder rose on the air and capture their fragrance with my Turkish delight and rosehip syrup recipes. There are plenty of greens packed full of vitamins, which can all be sizzled down with garlic into a healthy side dish and look out for sloe berries and crab apples as the months start to cool.

GUELDER ROSE

VIBURNUM OPULUS August to November

By midsummer the guelder rose is in full blossom and brightens every hedgerow, immediately recognisable for its ring of perfect white flowers encircling a cluster of smaller blooms that will eventually ripen into fruit. You might be wise to make a note of where these flower rings grow to ensure a victorious harvest of the fruits later on, but the berries themselves are so bright and fragrant that any fool could find them. Look out for glistening, cardinal-red drupes, hiding under maple-shaped leaves that tend to block berry clusters from view; I usually crouch down and look directly up through the foliage to find the best hoards. Guelder rose plants can be found in hedges, scrub and woodland on chalky soils. They are common throughout Britain but rare in Scotland. The species is named after the Dutch province of Gelderland, where it is believed the snowball tree, a cultivar of the species, first originated.

While the fruits can be eaten raw in small quantities, they taste much better when simmered down into a jam or jelly. The berries are extremely juicy and will burst onto your hands when picked, so beware of cream coats and jumpers. I love adding them to my hedgerow jelly recipe as they bring a fragrant sweetness to the flavour.

BLACKTHORN or SLOE

PRUNUS SPINOSA October to November

Discovering a hoard of fat sloes is one of autumn's greatest delights and in milder seasons I've even found a few growing right up to Christmas. While the berries can appear as early as September, resist the temptation to harvest before they are fully ripened; they begin their lives tinged with green and slowly develop into a dark Prussian blue. The task of picking can be painful if the forager has little patience; blackthorn is made up of thick branches covered in solid spikes, so it's worth taking some time. They can be found in most hedgerows and thickets across Britain (except those in acidic peat soils) and can grow up to 4m tall and 4m wide. As a shrub, it provides excellent shelter for nesting birds as well as nutritious winter food, so always try to leave a few berries behind.

Sloe gin is one of my favourite winter drinks and is ridiculously easy to make. Try following my recipe for dam sloe gin, which uses wild damson plums to complete the flavour. The berries can also be added to my hedgerow jelly with other wild fruits, or they can be simmered down into a gloopy syrup to accompany puddings and ice cream.

Winter Slider
page 214

Dam
Sloe Gin
page 210

BARBERRY

BERBERIS VULGARIS August to September

This little shrub is not native to Britain, but has found a way to grow across most of the country after escaping from gardens and naturalising itself; it pops up in hedges, woodland clearings and roadsides on most soils. The leaves are oval-shaped and cluster around yellowish twigs covered in three-pronged spikes; the flowers grow in small, yellow clusters. Bright red and sausage-shaped, the berries grow up to 12mm long and are high in vitamin C; with a pleasantly acidic taste they are a popular ingredient in Iranian cuisine, particularly in wedding dishes as a symbol of the fact that even the perfect life together will have its sour days. Look out for other members of the *Berberis* genus, which are all edible but can vary from sweet to dry and bitter.

Barberry seeds have a high pectin content so they are great for adding to jams and jellies to ensure a solid wobble; try popping a few in my hedgerow jelly recipe to see how the flavour changes. When pressed they also make a great substitute for lemon juice and the young leaves and buds are equally nutritious and great to sprinkle over salads in small amounts. Try adding fresh barberries, pistachios and saffron to rice for an exotic side dish.

Wild Rose Lokum
page 232

DOG ROSE

ROSA CANINA August to November

By late summer the aroma of dog roses starts to catch on the wind and my senses are overwhelmed by that deep infusion of lemons, violets and nasturtiums that can only be the delicate scent of rose. The wild rose is smaller and more humble than its cultivated cousin, but no less intense in colour, ranging from marshmallow whites to pinks and vivid purples. Found in hedges, woodland edges and scrub throughout Britain, the stems are covered in small, hooked thorns and pinnate leaves. Once the flowers have finished their bloom, they transform into orangey-red rosehips. They are a great source of vitamin C and a favourite autumn food for birds and small mammals; look to harvest these after the first frost.

If a good population can be found, the exquisite flavour of wild rose petals can be captured and used to make jam, jellies and lokum (Turkish delight). Rosehips are always in plentiful supply, but they do contain lots of fine hairs that can irritate the stomach when eaten raw. Try simmering them down into a syrup, a regular spoonful of which will give you a healthy dose of vitamins through the colder months. They can also be added to soups, or used to make a herbal tea or delicious country wine.

Rosehip
Syrup

page 226

CRAB APPLE

MALUS SYLVESTRIS August to December

Finding a crab apple tree can be a good challenge, not because they are uncommon, but because they grow alone, often being the only one of its kind in an entire woodland. We once had a fantastic crab apple bush in the front garden of our old house; we used to watch the house sparrows hopping about between the branches, gobbling insects. Growing up to 10m high in old woods and hedgerows on calcareous soils, the name comes from its 'crabbed' appearance from the gnarling and twisting of its twigs with growth; the flowers unfurl up to 4cm in diameter with clusters of white petals. The fruit is immediately recognisable as a small, acid green apple, most often fallen to the ground where it is devoured by hungry voles and badgers.

Crab apples are not pleasant to eat raw, but when cooked they make excellent jams and jellies due to their high pectin content; the jelly is a particularly good accompaniment to sweet breads and cheeseboards. Home brewers may also enjoy pressing the apples to make a sharp cider and, once simmered and sugared, they make a great addition to fruit pies.

BLACKCURRANT

RIBES NIGRUM July to August

Here's another of my favourite Latin scientific names, as *Ribes* was the inspiration for the blackcurrant drink Ribena when it was invented in 1938. Commonly found in gardens and allotments, the wild blackcurrant grows throughout Britain in woodlands and hedgerows on all but the poorest of soils. The leaves are wide and toothed with three to five lobes, the underside of which produce a strong aroma when rubbed between the fingers. Each flower bears five whitish petals tinted with greens and pinks; by midsummer these have developed into glossy, purple berries. Due to their high vitamin C content, blackcurrants were a favourite crop during WWII when exotic citrus fruits could not be so easily obtained.

Superbly sweet and juicy, blackcurrants are wonderful raw but are usually used in a number of other recipes, particularly pies, jams and jellies. The possibilities are almost endless with this little fruit; try adding them to compotes, summer pudding, Eton mess, black forest gateau, sorbet, tarts, cheesecakes and crumbles; the blackcurrant truly captures the flavour of summer.

GOOSEBERRY

RIBES UVA-CRISPA July to September

Gooseberries always remind me of a pick-your-own farm near my home, where I spent many sun-drenched afternoons as a child filling baskets with more plant matter than would ever fit in the fridge. The gooseberry is rarely seen in supermarkets, but it has a wonderful flavour of its own and the traditional gooseberry fool pudding, made with stewed gooseberries and custard, is inescapably British. Growing in woodlands and hedgerows across Britain, the gooseberry shrub bears many branches with sharp spines to defend its precious fruit. The berry itself resembles a greenish-yellow or dark red beach ball, filled with edible seeds.

When fully ripe the gooseberry can be eaten raw on the spot – a delightful treat on a warm August day. Alternatively, try concocting your own gooseberry fool using sugar, vanilla and cream, or utilise the high pectin content and make a summer jam with elderflower. They can also be used in place of most other berries, such as in crumbles, tarts, cakes, pies, cobblers, sorbet and strudel.

COMMON POPPY

PAPAVER RHOEAS July to September

Whenever I've sought to harvest poppy seeds, at least one person will ask me if they are dangerous due to their opiate connections. While opium does originate from the poppy flower, it is not from the wild poppy native to Britain, but the exotic species *Papaver somniferum*, whose Latin name literally means 'sleep-inducing'. English poppy seeds are harmless and the red flower is quite beautiful, producing a shower of seeds that are ready to harvest when the head has become heavy and broken the stem, allowing its 'pepper-pot' design to disperse the seeds nearby; when taking seeds for myself I always try to disperse a few more to help each poppy reproduce. Growing on disturbed ground, roadsides, arable fields and waste ground, the poppy can be found throughout Britain and is an important species for our bees and butterflies.

Poppy seeds bring a wonderful crunchiness to cakes, biscuits and pastries and their oil can theoretically be pressed out and used in cooking. They also make a great addition to hot curries and Indian dishes, or sprinkle over breads and breadsticks. Try adding the seeds to my lemon and marmalade cake, decorated with mallow flowers for a taste of summer.

Lemon, Marmalade & Poppy-seed Cake

page 244

HOP

HUMULUS LUPULUS July to September

Before the popularisation of hops in the production of beer, the drink's distinct flavouring was usually obtained from other wild plants, such as dandelion, burdock, ground ivy and heather. Its use was first documented in northern France in the year 822, when a chubby abbot wrote about the gathering of wild hops to make beer, but today they are grown commercially in hop gardens, where they are trained along string to ensure an efficient harvest. For home brewing enthusiasts, the hop plant can be found in hedgerows and thickets throughout England and Wales, supporting itself by twisting around other plants like hedge bindweed. Leaves are large with three to five lobes and the flowers grow in clustered cones, much like a small, green pine cone.

To make beer, the female flowers must be gathered unfertilised and dried. Their flavour adds an important citrusy bitterness to the beer and the dried flowers can be kept for many months before use. Alternatively, gather young hops before the end of May and steam with asparagus and a little butter.

MEADOWSWEET

FILIPENDULA ULMARIA June to September

Also known as the Lady of the Meadow, this aromatic flower has historically been associated with strong or significant women. Fans of Alan Garner's children's novel *The Owl Service* will recognise the figure Blodeuwedd ('flower face'), a woman of Welsh myth who was created out of oak blossom, broom and meadowsweet. With its strong, sweet smell it was also a popular flower for strewing on floors before cleaning standards were raised, with meadowsweet being a particular favourite of Queen Elizabeth I in sixteenth-century Britain. Found in wet meadows, ditches, streams and riverbanks, it grows on wet ground throughout the country reaching 2m in height. Leaves are oval and toothed and the flowers are heavily scented, creamy white and frothy, like the top of a cappuccino.

Aside from its olfactory properties, meadowsweet is delicious in cooking and brings a light almond flavour to sweet dishes. The flowers and leaves can be used dry or fresh to flavour wines, spirits, vinegar and honey mead, or they can be combined with elderflower to make a flavoured syrup for drinks and puddings. Alternatively, pop the flower into stewing fruit for a light summer crumble, or add to jams for an almondy tang.

SWEET VIOLET

VIOLA ODORATA March to September

This delicate purple wildflower has gained a romantic reputation throughout history, most famously with French revolutionary Napoleon who, after being defeated at the Battle of Waterloo, was allowed to visit the grave of his first wife Joséphine one last time. On seeing her resting place he discovered sweet violets growing there and picked a few; these same flowers were found in a locket around his neck when he died. With their sugary scent and vibrant petals, it's no wonder the violet has become so cherished and foragers can seek them out in shady meadows, woodlands, hedgerows and scrub throughout southern Britain. Leaves are toothed and shaped like kidneys; the flower head itself is symmetrical, bearing two petals on each side and one larger petal at the bottom.

Although sweet violets are classed as stable, many other wildflowers are in decline and it is best to only pick violets if a large population can be found. The flowers can be simmered down into a syrup to mix with prosecco or cocktails, or scatter them fresh over fruit salads, ice cream and other puddings. They can also be crystallised using egg white and sugar and used to decorate cakes.

COMMON NETTLE

URTICA DIOICA March to May

There are few people in Britain who won't be acquainted with the nettle; delicious and healthy as they are, the leaves and stems are covered in tiny stinging hairs and it's a rite of passage for small children to fall into a nettle patch and reappear covered in a blotchy rash. *Urtica dioica* refers to the common stinging nettle, but look out for the red dead-nettle (*Lamium purpureum*) and white dead-nettle (*Lamium album*), both of which are just as edible but do not sting. The seeds inside the flowers of white dead-nettle grow in pairs and my brother-in-law told me the story of how the seeds are actually elf shoes that are hung up in nettle flowers to keep tidy. All three types of nettle can be found throughout the year, but their leaves taste the best when picked between March and May. Look for them in hedgerows, woodlands, meadows, roadsides and waste ground, common across the country and always easy to find.

Cook young leaves and shoots like spinach, sautéeing in butter, garlic and salt for extra flavour, or add the leaves to hot soups, sauces and stews. Nettles make an excellent home brewed beer and when left to settle will produce a clear, russet draught with a wonderful wild tang.

Garlicky Greens
page 220

GOOD KING HENRY

CHENOPODIUM BONUS-HENRICUS April to July

Once grown in cottage gardens as a substitute for spinach and asparagus, it is now rarely eaten in Britain except by foragers and gardeners who are aware of its uses. Growing up to 60cm in height, the leaves are large and triangular, with small green flowers growing on a terminal spike. It is usually found on pastures, meadows, farmyards and roadsides on nitrogen-rich soils throughout Britain and is best picked in late spring when, as a perennial plant, it will provide fresh leaves year after year.

The leaves can be eaten raw in salads or cooked in the same way as spinach; young shoots are sweeter and can be steamed like asparagus. The clustered flower buds can be sautéed in butter with garlic and a little nutmeg for an excellent side dish.

FAT HEN

CHENOPODIUM ALBUM March to October

As the name might suggest, this was once used as a rich feed for chickens as it is full of protein, iron, calcium and vitamin B1. Although similar to its cousin good king henry, the flower buds are much whiter and fat hen is an annual plant, meaning the entire plant will grow, seed and die within a one year cycle. The leaves can vary in shape but will often form an oval with toothed edges and the seeds are marked with a crisscross pattern, like a brussel sprout ready for Christmas dinner. It grows on waste ground, cultivated land and farmyards on nitrogen-rich soils throughout Britain.

Young leaves can be cooked and eaten like spinach, but unlike good king henry, it is not recommended to eat them raw. They make a healthy addition to soups and stews when chopped.

WINTER CRESS OR YELLOW ROCKET

BARBAREA VULGARIS March to November

A member of the mustard family, winter cress has a sharp, hot taste (similar to watercress) and can be found in meadows, hedgerows, ditches, riverbanks and damp waste ground throughout Britain. Leaves at the base of the plant are large and lobed, while those at the top are smaller with crinkled edges. The flowers are buttercup yellow and grow in clusters. The name *Barbarea* originates from Saint Barbara, the patron saint of miners and artillerymen, as winter cress was once used on battlefields to soothe wounds caused by explosions – I've always thought that this compliments the alternative name, 'yellow rocket', quite nicely.

Although once grown as an early salad vegetable in Britain, it is no longer cultivated in the same way and the more commonly used watercress now provides the hot tang that livens up egg sandwiches. The leaves make an excellent addition to salads but can also be cooked like spinach, while the flower shoots can be steamed or stir-fried like broccoli.

WATERCRESS

RORIPPA NASTURTIUM-AQUATICUM April to November

Found in the shallowest patches of ditches, brooks and streams throughout Britain, wild watercress has creeping hollow stems that float upwards to flower near the water's surface. Leaves are dark green with rounded leaflets and the flowers are white and arranged in loose clusters. Farmed watercress is usually found on supermarket shelves, where it is sold in little plastic pots to grow at home; while still tasty, the wild version is much more rewarding to find and, if unharvested, will grow up to 4ft in fresh running water.

With its punchy, peppery taste, watercress adds heat to any salad, soup or sandwich and is full of both iron and vitamin C. Blend with peas, mint and sour cream for a fantastic sauce to accompany mackerel, scallops and other seafood, or create a delicious salad with watercress, pomegranate seeds, walnuts, mozzarella and balsamic glaze. Be aware of the environment in which your watercress is growing; avoid harvesting from water near livestock and always wash thoroughly to ensure the plant is clean. If in doubt, only use wild watercress in soups and other cooked dishes.

CUCKOOFLOWER OR LADY'S SMOCK

CARDAMINE PRATENSIS March to June

This pretty, pale flower takes its name from the time it blossoms, when the cuckoo begins its clockwork song. The nickname Lady's Smock may refer to the pinkish-lilac colour of its petals, which form a slightly cupped shape like that of a lady's skirt, but there are other, more raunchy suggestions of how the name was given, usually to do with frivolous youths frolicking in spring meadows. Indeed, the Latin name *pratensis* means meadow or grassy area and the flower can usually be found in damp pastures on rich soils throughout the country. Growing up to 60cm tall, it is a favourite food of the orange tip butterfly and is also thought to be sacred to fairies – so be careful.

Once used as an alternative to watercress, cuckooflower shares the same hot, peppery taste and makes a great addition to salads, soups and sandwiches.

SWEET CICELY

MYRRHIS ODORATA April to July

An aromatic plant with frothy, white flowers, sweet cicely's scientific name celebrates its pungent aniseed taste and smell with reference to the strongly scented oil myrrh, a valuable commodity from Asia. It grows throughout the hedgerows, woodlands and meadows of northern Britain, particularly near mountainsides and human settlements on neutral to acidic soils. The leaves are fern-like with lots of pinnate, wedge-like fronds. The flowers grow like upside-down umbrellas, with green-brown fruits developing later in the season.

For lovers of aniseed (heathens), sweet cicely seed pods make a fantastic mid-ramble treat and can be chewed or sucked to release the flavour. The leaves can also be eaten; their sweet flavour can be used to soften sharp fruits like cooking apples and raspberries. The young root can also be harvested and used like a parsnip.

ALEXANDERS

SMYRNIUM OLUSATRUM November to April

Like cats, cabbages and indoor plumbing, alexanders were brought over to Britain by the Romans and are native to the Mediterranean. An aromatic plant with dark, shiny leaves and bright yellow flowers, it can be found in hedgerows, woodlands and meadows near the sea, particularly along the coasts of southern Britain where it can grow up to 1.5m tall.

One of the best plants to forage in winter, alexanders are best collected before the flowers open. Try to find leaf stems that have been blanched pink by the surrounding vegetation and discard any deep green parts before boiling or steaming the stems like asparagus. Serve with salted butter. I've also heard this plant makes a great additive to a gin and tonic, either by infusing like sloe gin or making a syrup, which will taste a little like liquorice.

GROUND ELDER

AEGOPODIUM PODAGRARIA April to June

Although disliked by gardeners, the invasive nature of ground elder means that it is readily available and abundant throughout Britain, particularly in woodlands, hedgerows, gardens and waste ground near human settlement. Growing up to 1m tall, it has a similar frothy, white flower to sweet cicely, but the leaves are oval shaped with toothed margins.

Young leaves and shoots can be added to soups and salads, or sautéed with butter and garlic to create a spinach-like side dish. The leaves have a rather sharp flavour and can also be added to dhals and curries for extra greenery. Try to gather foliage before the flowers bloom to ensure a fresher flavour.

HOGWEED OR COW PARSNIP

HERACLEUM SPHONDYLIUM April to June

Found throughout Britain from late spring to early summer, hogweed grows in hedges, woodland and roadside verges and comes from the same family as fennel, ground elder and cow parsley. With downy veined leaves and white umbrella-shaped flowers, it is not to be confused with its toxic sibling giant hogweed (*Heracleum mantegazzianum*) which can grow up to 5m tall with enormous flowers. The Latin word *Heracleum* refers to the large size of each part of the plant, including wide leaves and a chunky stalk; however, unlike the giant variety, common hogweed will reach only 1.5m in height.

Young shoots and leaves can be cooked and eaten like spinach or steamed like asparagus.

BORAGE

BORAGO OFFICINALIS May to September

Also known as starflower due to its pretty shape, borage has traditionally been used to garnish fruit cups like Pimms, together with mint and woodruff. The green parts have a fresh, cucumber-like taste, while the sky-blue flowers are sweet and sugary. It tends to grow near human settlement on arable fields, grassy areas and free-draining soils and can be found throughout Britain. The leaves are almost blue-green and oval–shaped and children can pop the flowers into vinegar to turn it blue! The whole plant can reach up to 60cm in height.

Young leaves and flowers make a tasty addition to salads when chopped, or they can be sautéed with garlic and butter as a side vegetable. The flowers can also be crystallised and used to decorate cakes or biscuits.

WILD MARJORAM

ORIGANUM VULGARE April to September

Wild Marjoram is one of my favourite summer herbs, not only due to its pizza-like aroma, but also because it attracts an array of beautiful butterflies. Despite the Latin name, it is not to be confused with oregano, the Central American herb *Lippia graveolens* found on supermarket shelves that is similar in taste and scent. Marjoram grows in wondrous clusters along scrub, grassland and hedgerows on chalky soils, particularly abundant in southern Britain and blossoming into pink flowers that have the same aromatic quality as the leaves; these are small and slightly hairy with tall stems.

A popular addition to Greek and Mediterranean cookery, wild marjoram is a wonderful herb and worth drying to keep a full stock throughout the year; when doing so, try to pick stems without flowers in order to leave enough blossom for the pollinators. Add fresh or dried to stews, soups, pasta sauces, risottos and pizza, or infuse a few leaves in sugar to create a unique ingredient for the kitchen cupboard.

YARROW

ACHILLEA MILLEFOLIUM May to October

Yarrow has been used for cooking and medicine for hundreds of years across many countries and, like bog myrtle and ground ivy, was once used to flavour beer before hops became more popular. Found in meadows, pastures, hedgerows and most grassy places throughout Britain, the plant has white flower clusters and long, feathery leaves. In New Mexico it is called *plumajillo*, meaning 'little feather' and the Latin word *millefolium* refers to the numerous tiny leaves that line the outside of each stem.

Aside from its culinary uses, yarrow is famous for its healing properties in medicine; the leaves can be dried to make a tea, which is thought to cure colds, boost circulation and help digestion. Young leaves have a sweet but slightly bitter taste and can be chopped into salads, cooked like spinach or added to soup.

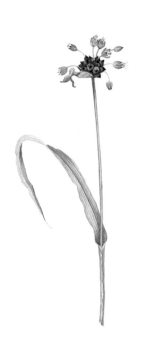

SAND LEEK

ALLIUM SCORODOPRASUM July to September

Also known as the rocambole, from the Danish word *rockenbolle* meaning 'rock onion', the sand leek belongs to the same family as the onion, garlic, shallot and chive. Consequently, the plant can be used in the same way as garlic, with the same delicious flavour but a little milder. It grows on banks and rough grassland on rocky soils in northern Britain; the stems are long and straight with flat leaves and the flowers grow in pink, white or purple bells, arranged in clusters and enclosed in a papery sheath. The flowers then develop into plump bulbils which can also be used like garlic.

Both the flower bulbils and underground bulbs can be used to conjure a mild garlicky infusion. Try roasting and swirling into mashed potato, or slowly fry the bulbs and add them to a creamy butternut squash tart.

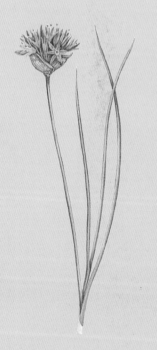

CHIVES

ALLIUM SCHOENOPRASUM All year

A familiar sight in most allotments and vegetable gardens, the chive is a most useful plant for people and bees alike. Found on grassland and dry, rocky soils throughout Britain, it is often inhabited by fat bumblebees who love delving into the vivid purple flowers that sit atop long, hollow stems. With its garlicky taste and aroma, it is unsurprising that in Romani culture dried chives are placed around the house to ward off evil, just as one might ward off vampires with garlic. Similarly, they are often deliberately planted in gardens to discourage leaf-nibbling insects.

Fresh chives are full of flavour and, while they grow throughout the year, they taste best in the spring and summer months. Chop finely and add to cottage cheese, baked potatoes, soups, sauces and omelettes, or chop roughly and sprinkle over salads and open sandwiches. I make fresh cheese with the milk from our goats and swirl in fresh chives and cracked black pepper. The flowers taste just as delicious as the leaves and can be rinsed thoroughly and popped into salads to add a flush of colour.

WILD PARSNIP

PASTINACA SATIVA November to March

The Romans thought parsnips were an aphrodisiac and eagerly cultivated them into the garden vegetable planted today; the Latin *sativa* means 'cultivated'. With their sweet flesh and pleasant flavour, they were also used as a sweetener before the arrival of cane sugar in Europe. The parsnip roots sleep underground beneath an aromatic plant with tall, hollow stems and toothed leaves. The flowers form a yellow umbrella up to 10cm in diameter. Found on roadsides, waste ground and meadows on chalky soils, they are common in southeast Britain but do not often grow elsewhere.

Wait until the first frost to unearth wild parsnips from the ground, as the flesh will be more tender and sweet. Do not expect the chubby kind of parsnip one might find in the supermarket; the wild variety is rather spindly, but still worth harvesting if a good patch can be found. Try finely slicing and frying them up with other root vegetables to make crisps, or chop and sauté with garlic for an excellent side dish.

SALSIFY

TRAGOPOGON PORRIFOLIUS September to March

Doesn't salsifysound like a a spell that Harry Potter would say? Possibly one that turns your victim into a Spanish dancer or tomato-based dip. Uncommon in Britain, it can only really be found in the southeast, usually in grassland, waste ground and old cultivated soils with good drainage; it is thought that any wild specimens have probably escaped from a garden somewhere. The stem is long and straight with flattish leaves, while the flowers blossom in pretty purple florets. Not to be confused with goat's beard (*Tragopogon pratensis*), which can be eaten in the same way but bears a yellow flower.

If you are fortunate enough to stumble upon a patch of salsify, it's the long, white roots that hold the flavour. Once dug up, these roots can be peeled carefully, then boiled or steamed to be served with a little butter, garlic, chilli and salt as a side dish.

GOAT'S BEARD

TRAGOPOGON PRATENSIS September to October

Similar in appearance to salsify (*Tragopogon porrifolius*), goat's beard has a bright yellow flower and long, pointed leaves, but the root is brown rather than white. The rural name 'Jack-go-to-bed-at-noon' originates in the flowers, which close up at midday. It can be found on pastures, meadows, hedgerows and sand dunes throughout England and Wales, but is rarer in Scotland and Ireland.

The tap roots can be dug up, peeled and eaten in the same way as salsify. Alternatively, the stems and young buds can be steamed like asparagus and young leaves can be added to soups and salads.

Pink Dandelion Wine

page 222

DANDELION

TARAXACUM OFFICINALE All year

A familiar flower to all growing up on the playing fields of Britain, I begrudge those who label the dandelion a mere weed. With its bright golden petals and fluffy 'clockwork' seed heads developing later in the season, it brightens up the darkest, scrappiest patches of ground and provides food for precious pollinators. Found on roadsides, lawns, river banks, waste ground, pastures and meadows throughout Britain (pretty much anywhere grassy), it grows all year round, but is best for foraging from April to June. The leaves are pointed and deeply toothed and the flowers look like little suns.

Due to their abundance, harvesting the dandelion is a simple and joyful task. Try to collect the flower heads early in the morning to ensure the freshest flavour; these have a delicate taste and can be used to make my pink dandelion wine. Young flower buds can also be pickled like capers and sprinkled over pizza and the young leaves can be eaten raw in salads or sautéed with butter like spinach. The root can also be cooked like parsnips and eaten as a side vegetable, or it can be roasted and ground to make an intriguing coffee substitute. Dandelions also produce ethylene, which helps to ripen fruit when placed nearby.

Orange & Dandelion Biscuits

page 240

FIELD BLEWIT or BLUE LEG

LEPISTA SAEVA October to December

One of the later species to appear as the colder months tighten their grip, the field blewit is one of our most well-known species of edible mushroom. It grows in pastures and grassy places, often forming magnificent fairy rings in large numbers and can be found across Britain. The fruiting body has a pale beige cap which at first grows concave, then flattens out with age. With pinkish gills and a beautiful lilac-blue stem, the flesh is thick and whitish with a strong aroma and flavour.

An excellent addition to meat and fish dishes, this mushroom can also be used to bulk up soups, stews and casseroles. Although the flavour is strong and tempting, it can cause slight digestive problems to a few people, so first-time consumers should try only a little chunk to check the blewit agrees with them. Avoid picking in wet weather, as they are rather porous and absorb rainwater, which will then leak out into cooking and dilute an otherwise tasty meal. Preserve under olive oil or cider vinegar.

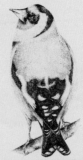

THE RARITY OF WILD FLOWERS

I know a bank where the wild thyme blows,
Where oxlips and the nodding violet grows,
Quite over-canopied with luscious woodbine,
With sweet musk-roses and with eglantine.
William Shakespeare, *A Midsummer Night's Dream*

Rummaging through the dusty shelves of a second-hand bookshop, I love hunting down old books on foraging simply to discover how much our landscape has changed within the last century. A look back over the last 30, 40 or 50 years reveals that most of these volumes will contain advice on eating species that have since declined so rapidly that they are endangered and protected, and no ethical forager would even consider sneaking a handful. Sea kale, oyster plant, spiked star of Bethlehem and sea holly are among those once celebrated as forageable delights, but their rarity now means they must not be harvested, for the sake of the delicate ecosystems in which they play their part. That doesn't, however, mean that these plants cannot be enjoyed from afar. Below are five once-edible British wildflowers (that are now under our protection) and a glance into their close connection with our environmental and social history. Get in touch with your local Wildlife Trust to find out how you can help wildflowers flourish in your area, or sow your own wildflowers with native seed mixes available from charities like Grow Wild and Friends of the Earth.

PRIMROSE *PRIMULA VULGARIS*

Can there be any greater sight than the primrose when we are longing for the warm days of spring? Found in woodland clearings and hedgerows, the primrose blossoms in happy shades of lemon yellow, pinks and purples and symbolises early youth, innocence and fear in the language of flowers. It is a native plant well distributed across the country, but its decline and vulnerability to habitat loss and climate change means they should always be left to grow wild in the ground. Did you know that the name derives from the Latin for 'first rose' of the year? Folklore claims the red and purple flowers develop when the primrose is planted upside-down and in Norse lore, it is the sacred flower of Freya, the goddess of love. Primroses are also the favourite food of the caterpillars of Duke of Burgundy butterflies, a rare species listed on the UK Biodiversity Action Plan – even more reason to let them be.

COWSLIP *PRIMULA VERIS*

A cousin of the common primrose, the cowslip grows in yellow pasta-like tubes and is another welcome sign that spring is on its way. In English folklore it is associated with floral weddings and May Day garlands, although the name 'cowslip' stems from a far less elegant premise; the Old English *cuslyppe* means 'cowpat', from which cowslips would often spring up when they were common in the wild.

Due to over picking and habitat loss, particularly ancient woodlands, traditional meadows and hedgerows, the cowslip has suffered severe declines and is now difficult to find in abundance. They were popular in Elizabethan gardens and were believed to be favoured by nightingales; for those wanting to seduce a loved one, you could try washing your face with milk infused with cowslips, or you could dazzle them with your crazy wildflower knowledge (a more successful method, in my experience).

EARLY PURPLE ORCHID *ORCHIS MASCULA*

One of our earliest flowering orchids, this species stands a little taller than the fresh grasses of spring and blooms frothy with violet petals. The scent of its first blossom is greater than any of its edible properties, but sadly this once-common plant has been depleted by modern farming and urban development and is far less abundant than it once was. Shakespeare knew these orchids as 'long purples'; in *Hamlet*, it is one of the flowers Ophelia weaves into her garland before drowning herself in the river:

> There is a willow grows aslant a brook
> That shows his hoar leaves in the glassy stream.
> There with fantastic garlands did she come,
> Of crowflowers, nettles, daisies and long purples,
> That liberal shepherds give a grosser name
> But our cold maids do dead men's fingers call them.

CORNFLOWER *CENTAUREA CYANUS*

Now classified as a Priority Species in the UK Biodiversity Action Plan, the cornflower was once considered a farmland weed but has almost been wiped out by intensive agricultural practices. In folklore, it was worn by young men who found themselves in love; if the blossom faded too quickly, he would have to accept his love was unrequited. It is perhaps most famous as one of the national symbols of Germany, due to the story of Queen Louise of Prussia. As she was fleeing Berlin and Napoleon's army, she hid her children in a field of cornflowers, keeping their silence by weaving wreaths of cornflowers to entertain them. When Prussia was unified into Germany in 1871, the cornflower went on to become their national symbol. In the language of flowers, it represents wealth, prosperity and friendship.

DITTANDER *LEPIDIUM LATIFOLIUM*

A scarce plant in Britain, dittander can only usually be found in East Anglia, Wales and the south. It has historically been cultivated here as a peppery herb to be used in the same way as horseradish, but due to its rarity, you are much better off eating its supermarket alternative. A halophyte plant that thrives around saltwater, it grows in ditches, sea-walls and estuarine saltmarshes and plays an important role for pollinators in local ecosystems. In Himalayan cuisine, the spring leaves are prized as a delicacy.

WILDLIFE WATCH: MEADOWS

For those who delight in the dizzy flutter of pollinators, there is no better place to spend an afternoon than a healthy meadow. With swathes of long grasses and the bright blossoms of wildflowers, our meadows are alive with the circadian rhythms of bees and butterflies, who are drawn to our wildflowers and, in turn, help to pollinate many of the crops we buy in the supermarket. Butterflies like the dark green fritillary flit between the flowers of knapweed and thistles, while the marbled white feeds on sheep's-fescue, Yorkshire-fog and tor-grass. Diurnal burnet moths dance in the sun like hazard warnings, decorated with blood-red spots and glossy wings, just as dragonflies and damselflies weave their way through the forest of grasses like bejewelled messengers glinting in the sun.

Did you know there are 275 species of bumblebee in the world? There are 24 species living in Britain alone, feeding on sugary nectar and pollen inside flowers to gain energy. Sadly, in the last century, we have lost two native bees to extinction: Cullem's bumblebee and the short-haired bumblebee, although the latter is being reintroduced to Dungeness with positive results. Our bumblebees have suffered as wild meadows disappear, and deadly pesticides are used on our farmland, but we can help them by planting bee-friendly wildflowers in our gardens and public spaces. When out foraging, look for buff-tailed, white-tailed and garden bumblebees, who will be tumbling about the countryside from spring onwards.

There are six species of deer in Britain, four of which have been introduced, the fallow, sika, muntjac and Chinese water deer and two of which are native, the roe and red deer. The majority of these can be spotted grazing the sweet grasses of our meadows. However, though they are relatively large and

recognisable, their cautious nature often makes them difficult to find. Amazingly, roe deer were hunted to extinction during the eighteenth century in England, Wales and southern Scotland; their abundance today is mainly thanks to a successful reintroduction programme a century later.

Hidden in the depths of our wildflower labyrinths, the meadow is also home to some rodents and small mammals. The field vole is a common inhabitant and almost impossible to see, as is the harvest mouse who builds a spherical nest of woven material in the tops of the grasses. Most enchanting of all is the long-eared hooligan of the meadow, the brown hare; with golden fur and a pale belly, hares graze on vegetation and tree bark and bound through the grass in zigzags when disturbed. They are most visible in their springtime breeding season, when they perform their famous boxing matches; despite popular belief, these

fights are not between two competing males, but occur as a result of irritated females fending off pesky seducers.

With such a bustling array of flowers, pollinators, rodents and mammals, it comes as no surprise that our meadows are a fantastic place to birdwatch. Lapwings find safe spaces to nest on the ground, while goldfinches and other garden birds feed on the seeds of teasels, greater hawkbit, field scabious and sorrel. Lingering in the sky above, look out for birds of prey like buzzards and kites and the wavering hover of a kestrel hunting down rodents in the grasses below. They have excellent eyesight and ultraviolet vision, useful for locating voles who leave a trail of ultraviolet urine wherever they go. At dusk, keep an eye out for the silent ghost of a barn owl, whose heart-shaped face is perfectly engineered to collect and direct sounds towards the inner ears.

RECIPES

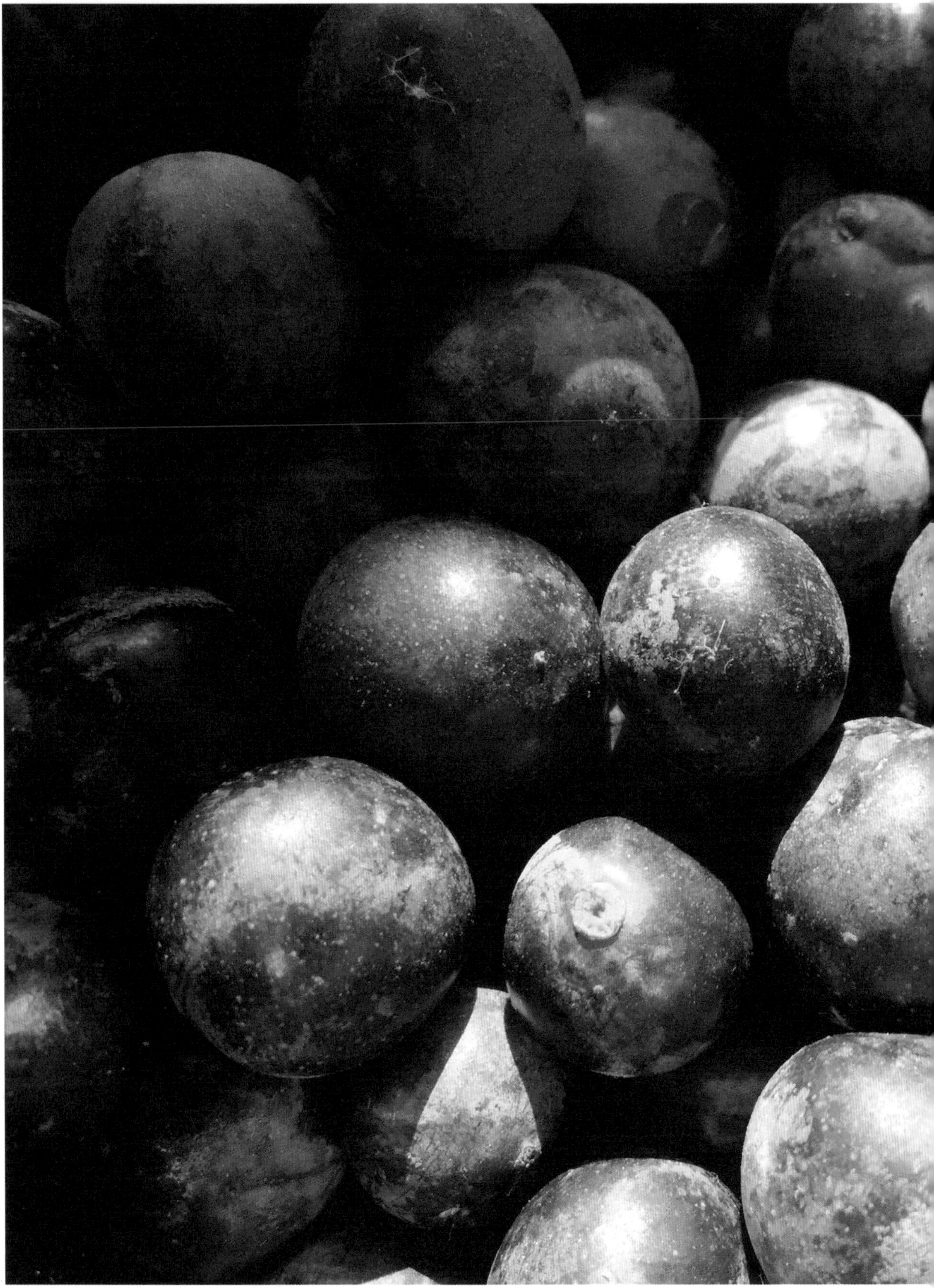

COOKING WITH FORAGED FOOD

An afternoon spent in the kitchen is the easiest way to fuel creativity, fend off the blues and fill the bellies of loved ones. Whether I'm huddled away in big jumpers on rainy November weekends, or enjoying a midsummer breeze through open windows and doors, I am yet to experience a mood that cannot be lifted with a little butter, sugar, cheese or garlic. While the art of foraging is rewarding in itself, it's even more satisfying to transform a basket of fresh plants into cordials, cakes and glistening jars of jam, which often allows you to enjoy your forage long after the plant has stopped growing outside.

Aside from the chance to fill your cupboards with lovely food, these recipes also make great gifts for birthdays, house sitters, or to thank that person who watered your plants while you were on holiday. Last Christmas I was given a jar of fresh orange curd and a bottle of vanilla brandy by two work colleagues, both made with love in their kitchens – it certainly beat another shampoo gift set. Foraging also enables you to create the greatest gift of all: cheap booze. However, bear in mind that it can be rather difficult to guess how alcoholic your concoctions are and if you value the longevity of your organs it may be worth investing in a cheap hydrometer online.

The key to brewing up things in the kitchen is to always save your jars and bottles. We've all drooled over those beautiful swing-top bottles and gingham-draped jar sets in home stores, but the truth is they are often overpriced and to buy enough for even one batch of jam will set you back. As Richard Mabey so wisely declared, foraging is essentially 'food for free', so by reusing old jars, you will find the hobby much more lucrative and environmentally friendly. Old labels can be easily removed with hot soapy water and new ones applied; I use blackboard paint to cover the tops of the lids and scrawl the contents on with a chalk pen. On each container, I also recommend adding the 'Made' date and the 'Consume by' date, as these are often very different and will help you keep track of your creations.

The following recipes are all vegetarian-friendly, and I always recommend using other ethical ingredients where possible, particularly free range eggs and organic produce. Not only is this better for the planet, it's better for the soul when you know your food has come from a good place. One last thing to mention: while I've used metric measurements and spoonfuls where possible, many of the ingredients used here are too weird to weigh, and I have never been able to work out what one 'cup' should equate to. I have therefore used 'mugs' to measure certain ingredients, as I feel confident every kitchen in Britain contains at least one standard-sized mug.

Dam Sloe Gin

A self-confessed Agatha Christie fan, I have always been intrigued by Miss Marple's famous damson gin and have done my best to lift it from the pages into my own kitchen. Gin has a devilish history of corrupting women who dared to drink alongside men in the eighteenth century; perhaps it's this reputation that makes it so tempting. This recipe is a variation on the traditional spirit, made by infusing blackthorn berries (sloes) and sugar into gin to create a crimson liqueur that conjures into the mind dusky forests and December nights. I've also added damsons, a small plum from the same family as the blackthorn that adds a deeper sweetness to the flavour. These can be found wild along country lanes and hedgerows. This recipe is perfectly timed for a Christmas treat; I usually find that if I gather the sloes as soon as they ripen around October, after two months of storage my sloe gin will be ready for the festive season. They are best to gather after the first frost, but even if it's been a particularly warm autumn they are still fine to collect as soon as they reach that lovely purpley-green stage. I like it neat or jazzed up in a prosecco cocktail. Credit goes to my bro-in-law Simon for thinking up the sharp title of this recipe.

750g sloe berries
250g damsons
500g caster sugar
2 litres gin

Sterilise a demijohn using a special steriliser like a Campden tablet. Rinse well, then pour in the gin and caster sugar, swirling together to dissolve the sugar. Next, rinse the sloes and damsons thoroughly under cold running water. Start by slitting one sloe berry with a sharp knife and popping it into the gin and sugar mixture, continuing until all the sloes have been added. Next, slice each damson in half and add these to the mixture; don't worry about including the stones as they will all be sieved out before drinking begins. Once all the fruit has been added, swirl the whole mixture vigorously and seal the demijohn with a cork. Continue swirling once a week and it will be ready for guzzling on Christmas day. To serve, use a sieve to strain out the sloe berries, which can be composted or used to make Winter Slider (p 216).

Wild Garlic & Cheese Scones

The smell of wild garlic in spring is one of my favourite woodland experiences and a sure sign that warmer weather is on the way. The leaves can be used in a multitude of ways, but I can't imagine anything nicer than a warm, garlicky scone oozing with cheese on the kitchen table. The cheese I've used in this recipe is Old Winchester, a vegetarian alternative to parmesan with a Gouda-like sweetness and a caramelised tang. It's my favourite way to create the earthy richness of parmesan without using animal products, but if you can't find this specific cheese, omnivores can simply exchange it for parmesan or Grana Padano to conjure similar flavours. I like these scones with plenty of butter, strong cheese and hedgerow jelly.

250g self-raising flour, sieved
Pinch of sea salt
1 tbsp dried thyme, chopped
1 tsp baking powder
60g salted butter
100g extra mature Cheddar, grated
10g Old Winchester cheese
100ml whole milk
30g Taleggio cheese
6 wild garlic leaves, chopped
1 tsp English mustard

Preheat the oven to 200°C and lightly grease a baking tray. Mix together the flour, salt, thyme and baking powder, ensuring ingredients are thoroughly combined. Cut the butter into small cubes and add to the bowl of flour, before rubbing the mixture together using your fingertips to create a breadcrumb-like texture. Add the Old Winchester and 60g of the grated Cheddar and stir well. Then, make a well in the middle of the bowl and pour in a little milk before stirring well. The aim is to keep adding dashes of milk until the mixture forms a soft but firm dough. Using your hands, add the Taleggio, wild garlic and English mustard and knead together. If the dough becomes a little sticky at this point, add a sprinkle of flour to firm it up. Next, lightly flour a smooth surface and roll out the cheesy dough to about one inch thick. Use a medium cutter (I sometimes use a mug) to cut out circles in the dough and place these on the baking tray. Glaze each circle by brushing the top with a little milk and sprinkle a little of the remaining grated Cheddar over each one before placing the tray in the oven. Bake for 12–15 minutes until golden brown.

Winter Slider

I really hate wasting food. Even though tart sloe berries aren't exactly fruit-salad-ready (and they can be given to pigs or compost heaps), their flavour is too lovely not to capture. This recipe uses the berries that I've strained from my dam sloe gin (p210) and uses them to whizz up a new concoction: sloe-infused cider. After a winter walk there is nothing I love more than a cold pint of cider by the fire in our local pub and this sloe cider (slider) adds a festive twist to a drink more often associated with pub gardens and festivals. Try to source cider from local breweries, as these have more unique and complex flavours. The resulting drink is tinted pink and with the infusion of gin it truly warms the soul against January frosts.

All the sloe berries removed
from your dam sloe gin
1 litre dry cider

Take a sterilised demijohn and pour in the cider. Separate the sloes out from the damsons if you haven't already and, without rinsing, pour them into the demijohn with the cider. Once all the sloes have been added, swirl the whole mixture vigorously and seal the demijohn with a cork. Continue swirling once a week and it will be ready in a month. To serve, use a sieve to strain out the sloe berries (which can be composted).

Hedgerow Jelly

This was one of the first things I learnt to make from forageable food. It's traditionally made to use up all the berries leftover at the end of the harvest, after sticky-fingered children have gorged all the blackberries and the birds have grown fat on rosehips. Most of the remaining berries are a little bit shrivelled and sorry-for-themselves by this point and a sweet jelly is a great way to capture their flavours before autumn descends into winter. It is worth keeping a jar back for Christmas as it makes a wonderful cheeseboard addition, particularly with sheep's cheeses like Manchego and Swaledale. Try using as many different fruits as you can, including sloes, damsons, rowan, blackberries, guelder rosehips, elderberries, haws, dog rosehips and wild plums. Just remember to leave some behind for the birds as they will need the sugar to keep going over winter.

500g mixed hedgerow berries
500g cooking apples
200ml cold water
Cane sugar, 100g per 100ml juice

Wash the fruit thoroughly with cold running water, picking out any leaves, bugs and bits of soil. Shake dry and pour into a large preserving pan, then wash and roughly chop the cooking apples into 1 inch cubes (without removing the core or peel) and add these to the pan. Add the cold water to the pan and simmer the whole lot until everything is soft and mushy. Give it a stir to check progress and then leave to cool. Take a jelly bag, tea towel or muslin cloth and transfer the mixture into it. Leave to strain overnight, ensuring you catch all the lovely juice in a clean bowl. At this point, traditionalists will insist the muslin bag is not squeezed; if you squeeze the juice from the muslin bag, the juice and future jelly will become cloudy. However, this doesn't affect the flavour and I find a squeeze of the bag results in much more juice – I prefer to have lots of cloudy jelly rather than a little bit of clear jelly! The next day, measure the fresh juice and add it to a clean preserving pan. For every 100ml of juice, add 100g of cane sugar to the pan and start to simmer over a low heat. Start to increase the heat until the mixture is boiling ferociously and then turn off the flame. Transfer quickly into warm, sterilised jars and allow to cool before leaving to set in the fridge.

Blackberry and Basil Syrup

Blackberries are the ultimate hedgerow berry. Even the sour ones are delicious raw, conjuring up warm afternoons in September, wandering along country paths in search of sweetness. This is a great recipe for fresh blackberry syrup, something a little different after the endless crumbles and cakes usually made in autumn. The syrup itself will keep for a couple of weeks, but if you want to make it throughout the year, simply freeze a few berries for later use. I've added basil to lift the flavour, but it also works well with wild thyme or any herb you might find in Mediterranean cuisine. Try drizzling over lemon sorbet or pour a little into prosecco bubbles for a cool autumn cocktail. Alternatively, freeze the syrup into ice cubes for an easy way to liven up drinks.

1kg blackberries
200g cane sugar
200ml water
Juice of 1 lime
1 mug fresh basil leaves

Wash the blackberries under cold running water and pour into a large preserving pan. Add the sugar, lime juice and water to the pan and simmer the whole lot for 15–20 minutes until the blackberries have softened to mush. Shred the basil leaves into the pan and simmer for another five minutes, then remove from the heat. Using a sieve with fine mesh, strain the syrup into a fresh bowl to remove the basil leaves and blackberry seeds. Transfer to a bottle and leave to cool. Once cooled, store in the fridge to thicken.

Garlicky Greens

Many of the plants found in this book are fresh greens waiting to be served up in the kitchen, hot and sizzling. My favourite way to eat foraged greens is with plenty of melted butter and garlic, perfect for a side dish to accompany roast dinners or any hot meal that's in need of a little greenery. The best thing about this recipe is that the 'greens' can be found throughout the seasons and include anything from the following list: lesser burdock, garlic mustard, sorrel, jewel weed, goosegrass, comfrey, common valerian, herb bennet, ground ivy, wild garlic, sea beet, common orache, sea purslane, black mustard, wild cabbage, common scurvy-grass, milk thistle, rosebay willowherb, nettle, good king henry, fat hen, winter cress, ground elder, hogweed, borage, yarrow and dandelion.

Knob of salted butter
4 shallots, sliced
3 garlic cloves, chopped
600g mixed greens
½ tsp dried wild marjoram
Sprinkle of sea salt and pepper

Heat the butter in a large pan until melted, then add in the shallots and chopped garlic. Gently fry until both are soft and sizzling, before adding in the mixed greens and sautéing until everything is soft. Sprinkle with the wild marjoram, salt and pepper to serve.

Pink Dandelion Wine

When the frosts of winter finally begin to thaw in March, dandelions are one of the first flowers to unfurl in the weakened sun. Although their seed 'clocks' were a most accurate way to tell the time as a child, for adults they can be used to create something a little more tempting. Dandelion wine is known for its unique and tangy flavour, but combined with the tart sweetness of raspberries it makes for a refreshing drink in late summer. Pick your dandelions on an early spring morning, when the flowers are in full blossom and the heads just starting to open. The final concoction should be drunk ice cold with a dash of lemonade for extra sparkle.

10 mugs dandelion heads
2.3 litres boiling water
2 lemons
2 limes
800g sugar
350g fresh raspberries
1 rounded tsp yeast

Wash the dandelion heads in cold running water, snipping off any green leaves where the head joined the stem and pop each head into a sterilised demijohn. Cover with the boiling water and leave to stand overnight. The next day, squeeze the contents through a tea towel or muslin cloth and combine with the lemon and lime juices, raspberries and sugar in a preserving pan. Heat gently and simmer for 25 minutes. Once the liquid has finished simmering, return it to the demijohn and cool to room temperature, around 25°C. Add the yeast and swirl the liquid until the yeast has dissolved and spread out. Leave to ferment, with an airlock, for 12 days. After this time, strain the liquid into swing-top bottles. For the first 24 hours, leave the swing-top resting on the bottle without securing, to reduce the chance of major fizz explosion. Seal the bottles and leave for at least six months before drinking.

PINK
DANDELION
WINE

Pesto Primavera

Nothing beats the soft texture of fresh, homemade pesto and it's not just there to jazz up pizza and pasta dishes; try combining this with sour cream for an aromatic dip, stir through buttery mashed potato or add a dollop to thick green soups. I've named this recipe after the Italian word for spring, as by using either wild garlic, nettles or garlic mustard, you should theoretically be able to make a fresh batch of pesto from the earliest, coldest days of spring until the first bright mornings of summer. Old Winchester cheese is my favourite vegetarian alternative to parmesan, but Cornish Quartz is much easier to find and extremely delicious, with an added crunch from the salt crystals ingrained in the cheese.

100g leaves from wild garlic,
nettle or garlic mustard
10 fresh basil leaves
60g Old Winchester cheese or
Cornish Quartz Cheddar, grated
50g pine nuts, toasted and chopped
140ml olive oil, plus extra
Sprinkle of sea salt

Wash your chosen leaves with cold running water and leave aside. When dry, pop the leaves, basil, cheese, pine nuts and sea salt in a food processor and blend together until everything is coarsely chopped. Start adding one glug of olive oil at a time to the processor and whizz until all the oil has been added or you are happy with the consistency. Transfer the mixture into a sterilised jar and, when full, cover the top with a layer of oil to seal it in. Use fresh or within a few weeks.

Rosehip Syrup

During World War II, when our supply of delicious citrus fruits was compromised by disrupted trading, the British government encouraged citizens to make their own rosehip syrup to ensure families could still maintain their vitamin levels. Rosehips are bursting with goodness and contain 50 per cent more vitamin C than the humble orange. In mild winters, I've discovered rosehips lingering in the hedgerow right up until new roses start blooming, but they are best collected in the autumn, when a bottle of rosehip syrup will keep your immune system boosted all through winter. Try drizzling this over porridge or pancakes, or stir into full fat yoghurt or rice pudding with a few slices of other autumn fruits, like pears or apples.

1kg wild rosehips
3 litres fresh water
500g brown sugar

Start by bringing two litres of water to the boil in a large pan and rinse the rosehips thoroughly under cold running water. Once rinsed, shake off any excess water and chop by hand to ensure each hip is broken down into a few pieces (you can use a food processor for this but I prefer the old-fashioned way). Once the water has boiled, remove from the heat and pour in the chopped rosehips. Allow to steep for 20-30 minutes and then use a jelly bag to strain out the rosehips while collecting the juicy water in a bowl. Be sure to gently squeeze the bag to ensure as much juice falls through as possible. Keep this juice aside and boil the last litre of the water. The reason for using two different batches of water is to capture the strongest flavour in the first two litres, then the last little bit of flavour will be concentrated in the last litre. If you want to quicken the process, all the water can be used at once but it may slightly diminish the subtlety of the rosehips. Remove the mush from the jelly bag and return it to the pan with the boiling water. Remove the pan from the heat and leave the mixture to steep once more, for another 30 minutes. Strain the liquid as before and add all the liquid together over a low heat to simmer (the mush can be added to the compost heap). Pour in the brown sugar and stir for five minutes to dissolve, before leaving to cool slightly and pouring into warm, sterilised bottles.

Puffball Risotto

With the aroma of wild marjoram and earthy Old Winchester, this mushroom risotto is a wonderful, hearty dish for early autumn evenings. I love using the puffball itself as a bowl, scooping out the inner flesh to bring flavour to the risotto before returning it to the ball for a funky way to dine. It's best to pop the hollowed out puffball into a bowl to add extra support and ensure the juices don't seep through, plus you can gobble up the outer flesh afterwards. Once again, I've used Old Winchester cheese as a vegetarian substitute for parmesan, but if you want to use the latter, a great way to add extra flavour is to cut the tough rind up into tiny cubes and mix them into the risotto. They are too hard to melt, but will soften into delicious chunks that fill each spoonful with even more wonderful cheesiness.

1 onion, chopped
3 garlic cloves, chopped
Glug of olive oil
1 puffball mushroom
300g arborio rice
200ml dry white wine
1 litre vegetable stock
100g Old Winchester cheese, grated
50g dried oyster mushrooms, chopped
Sprinkle of dried wild marjoram
Sea salt and pepper to season

Start by finely chopping the onion and garlic. Heat the olive oil in a medium sized stock pot and add the onion and garlic into the oil, frying gently for a few minutes until soft. Next, use a spoon or knife to carefully carve out the middle of the puffball mushroom, similar to scooping the seeds out of a pumpkin. Leave a thick wall so the puffball is still fairly solid but the hole is large enough to hold a portion of risotto, then place the hollowed puffball to one side. Take the scooped out flesh and weigh out 250g, then leave the rest aside for another recipe later in the week. Chop the measured flesh roughly into half-inch-thick chunks and add these to the onion and garlic. Cook gently for 8–10 minutes, on a low to medium heat until soft, then add the dry arborio rice and stir well for one minute. Add the white wine and mix thoroughly, allowing it to bubble for a few minutes until the alcohol has evaporated. Then add a third of the vegetable stock, mixing well until the rice has absorbed all the liquid and swollen slightly. Repeat twice more until all the stock has been absorbed and the risotto is looking plump and delicious. When the rice is cooked (taste testing essential), add the dried oyster mushrooms, wild marjoram and two thirds of the cheese. Season and mix through for a minute or two, then use a ladle to scoop the risotto back into the puffball mushroom. If you want to serve two dishes, simply slice the puffball in half to create plate shapes. Sprinkle over the rest of the cheese and serve.

Hazelnut and Cranberry Loaf

What could be dreamier than the smell of freshly baked bread floating through the kitchen? This sweet loaf is actually more like a hot cross bun in taste and texture, brimming with fruit and speckled with the crunch of fresh hazelnuts. Be sure to chop the cranberries quite small or they may weigh the loaf down, creating gaps and sinking to the bottom. I recommend baking this on rainy autumn afternoons with a murder mystery on in the background; my current favourite is Grantchester. This is a real comfort food, so serve warm with oodles of salted butter and hot tea.

160g brown sugar
130g salted butter
2 medium eggs, beaten
100g cranberries, chopped small
100g hazelnuts, chopped
225g plain white flour, sieved
1 tbsp baking powder
Pinch of sea salt

Preheat the oven to 190°C and thickly grease a 2lb loaf tin with butter. Cream together the sugar and butter in a bowl until smooth and fluffy and then beat in the eggs one at a time. When the mixture is well combined, add the chopped hazelnuts and cranberries and then sift in the flour, baking powder and salt. Fold everything together gently until the hazelnuts and cranberries are well dispersed. Pour the mixture into your greased loaf tin and bake for around 45 minutes. After 30 minutes, check to see if the top is burning (mine usually is); if so, add a layer of greaseproof paper to the surface and continue to bake. Allow to cool slightly before slicing and enjoy warm with a blob of butter.

Wild Rose Lokum

Don't be startled by the exotic sound of this recipe – lokum is just the Arabic word for that squidgy, scented cube of goodness we call Turkish Delight. I remember watching the 1988 BBC adaptation of *The Lion, the Witch and the Wardrobe* on video and finding the idea of Turkish delight unbelievably tempting after Edmund Pevensie is seduced by the White Witch with an enchanted box of the stuff. There's something about its sticky texture and fragrant taste that makes it truly special to devour. Real lokum is usually made with gelatine, but this recipe uses cream of tartar instead so the whole thing is vegan friendly. Try to pick the rose petals without damaging the rest of the flower, as they should hopefully still transform into hips later in the year. You will also need a sugar thermometer. Turkish delight makes a wonderful gift at Christmas or Easter and is the perfect way to capture the blissful aroma of wild roses; just remember to lightly dust your lokum with icing sugar to stop it sticking together.

For the rosewater
1 mug wild rose petals
2 mugs fresh water

For the lokum
425ml water
½ tbsp lemon juice
400g granulated sugar
½ tbsp cream of tartar
65g cornflour
Red food colouring (optional)
Almond oil for greasing
Icing sugar to dust

To make the rosewater, gently rinse your rose petals under soft running water and pop them in a glass heat-resistant bowl. Boil the fresh water and then pour gently over the rose petals, leaving to steep in the bowl for 20–30 minutes. Then use a piece of muslin or cheesecloth to pour the water into a warm, sterilised bottle, leaving the rose petals aside for the compost heap. After the rosewater has been used for this recipe, the rest can be stored in the fridge.

To make the lokum, start by placing 180ml of the water in a large stock pot over a medium heat with the lemon juice and sugar. Stir thoroughly until the sugar dissolves into the mixture and then insert the sugar thermometer so that it's hovering in the liquid rather than touching the bottom. Keep boiling the liquid until it reaches 115°C and then remove the pan from the heat. Leave to cool slightly.

Meanwhile, add the rest of the water to another large pot, along with the cream of tartar and cornflour and whisk well over a medium heat. Keep whisking until the mixture boils and it resembles a thick paste, then take it off the heat. Slowly pour in the sugary syrup a little at a time and keep whisking to ensure it blends in well. Then scrape down the sides of the pan to ensure all the sugar crystals are mixed in and stir for one or two minutes more. Pop it back over a medium heat and continue to stir until the mixture slowly comes to a boil. At this point, turn the heat down to its lowest setting and leave the mixture to simmer for an hour, stirring every few minutes to stop it sticking.

After an hour, turn off the heat and add in two teaspoons of your homemade rosewater; you can also add in a few drops of red food colouring if you want your lokum to be more vibrant, but I prefer a natural colour. Next, take a baking tin at least 5cm deep and grease it with almond oil. Line the tin with baking parchment and then grease that, too, to ensure the lokum will definitely not stick. Pour your gooey mixture into the tin and jiggle it to make sure it fills the corners, then leave to set for 6-8 hours. When it's ready, tip your lokum onto a surface lightly dusted with icing sugar and peel off the baking parchment to reveal all the surfaces. Cover every sticky surface with icing sugar and then use a pizza slicer (icing sugared) to cut your block of lokum neatly into cubes. Place each cube into a bowl of icing sugar and toss around to cover all sides, before arranging in a pile to serve after dinner.

Hawthorn Vinegar

The autumn hedgerow is one of the most diverse places to forage small fruits and the hawthorn tree is almost always carrying the heaviest harvest of berries. It doesn't take long to gather a small hoard and aside from jams and jellies, they also make a fantastic addition to vinegar. I've used cider vinegar in this recipe as it's my favourite kind, but you can also use malt, sherry or red wine vinegars. Hawthorn vinegar can be used in lots of dressings and sauces; my boyfriend combines it with wholegrain mustard and olive oil and sprinkles it over roasted vegetables and grilled halloumi.

300ml cider vinegar
1 mug hawthorn berries

Pour the vinegar into a 500ml bottle and leave the top open. Take your mug of haw berries and use a knife to gently slit each one, before popping them into the bottle with the vinegar. Keep adding the berries until your vinegar level reaches the top of the bottle. If you run out of berries before this point, simply top it up with a little more vinegar. Leave to infuse at kitchen temperature for 4–6 weeks.

Spiced Elderberry Buns

When one thinks of the elder tree, it's usually the flower that gains the most attention. The taste of elderflower is the taste of June and it's no surprise that everyone wants to capture the flavour in bottles of homemade cordial and champagne. But the fruit of the elder should not be overlooked; this recipe combines the darker flavour of berries with a twist of lemon, creating a swirly treat in the style of Chelsea buns. The important thing is not to let the buns burn, an incredibly easy thing to do and I have done on numerous occasions! The transformation from undercooked to overcooked takes place within a minute or two and, unlike bacon or marshmallows, they do not taste good burnt.

500g plain flour, sieved
Pinch of sea salt
7g dried yeast
300ml whole milk
50g salted butter
1 medium egg
200g fresh elderberries
75g demerara sugar
2 tsp mixed spice
25g unsalted butter
225g icing sugar
2-3 tbsp lemon juice

Sift the flour, salt and yeast together in a bowl and make a well in the middle using a spoon. In a saucepan, heat the salted butter until it has melted and add this, as well as the milk and egg, to the flour mixture. Using your hands, stir the whole mixture together until it forms a soft dough; you may need to add a little flour or milk depending on the consistency. Sprinkle a little flour onto a clean surface and spread out to create a non-stick area, then tip your dough mixture out. Knead the dough for five to ten minutes (depending on arm strength – it takes me ages) until the consistency is smooth and elasticated, but no longer sticky. Return the dough to the bowl and cover with a tea towel, then set aside at room temperature for an hour. Meanwhile, pour the elderberries into a preserving pan with a little water and simmer until the berries have softened to a juicy mush. Remove from the heat, add the sugar and mixed spice and stir well. In a separate pan, heat the unsalted butter until it has melted and leave aside. Once the dough has risen to twice its size, lightly flour a surface and tip the dough out. Roll out into a rough rectangle around ½cm thick and brush the exposed surface lightly with the melted unsalted butter. Then tip the elderberry mixture onto the surface and spread out evenly across the rectangle. Carefully roll the rectangle into a sausage so that the elderberry mix forms a spiral through the middle and, once secured, slice the sausage into 4cm slices. Place each slice on its side onto a greased baking tray and cover them all with a tea towel. Preheat the oven to 190°C and leave the slices to rise for 30 minutes. When risen, bake the slices for 20 minutes until they are golden brown and transformed into swirly buns and leave to cool. In a separate bowl, mix the icing sugar and lemon juice to form glacé icing and drizzle over every cooled bun until well coated.

Gorse Kick Mead

Mead can be one of the most sumptuous drinks when brewed properly and one that should never really be bought in a commercial supermarket. In Hampshire we have a local man who makes mead from his own honeybees and adds elderflower and hawthorn to create deep woodland flavours. I highly recommend sourcing local honey for this recipe; not only does it nourish your local environment and community, but all jars of honey taste different and it's wonderful to be able to capture the unique flavours of the landscape around you. This recipe was inspired by rambles across heather moors on hot days; gorse petals have a sweet, coconutty fragrance, but you do have to work a little harder to gather them as their thorns are a nightmare! Combined with the flavour of honey and gorse, the chilli is not particularly fierce but it does leave a warming sensation after the last drop is guzzled. This recipe makes 5–6 bottles.

1.2kg clear honey
1.9 litres fresh water
1 tsp dried yeast
2 mugs of fresh gorse petals
8 chillies, dried or fresh

Take a sterilised demijohn and pour in the honey, water, yeast, gorse petals and chillies. Stir thoroughly, either with a stick or by swirling the mixture around and then seal the opening with an airlock. Leave at room temperature for 4–6 weeks, or until the water in the airlock stops bubbling. If possible, transfer the mixture into bottles using a syphon, which means you can avoid the gorse petals and take out the clearest part of the liquid. If a syphon is not available, sieve the mixture slowly into bottles, taking care not to leave an air gap between the liquid and the bottle top. The mead will be a little cloudy at first but over time any residue will settle at the bottom of the bottle. Store the bottles in a cool, dark place for a year before drinking.

Orange and Dandelion Biscuits

Infused with the fresh flavours of dandelion and citrus, these make the perfect treat for Easter picnics and spring afternoon tea. Biscuits have always been one of my favourite indulgences, but the problem with buying a whole pack is knowing they're lurking in the cupboard, waiting for my self-discipline to crumble like a custard cream. It's a well known fact that homemade biscuits taste far better than the supermarket variety, but I've managed to perfect a method that allows me to bake just a few at a time and reduce the temptation to gorge. Once you've made the biscuit dough, simply roll it up into a cylinder, wrap in clingfilm and freeze. When you want to bake a few biscuits, take out your frozen cylinder and slice a few biscuit-sized slices off the end; bake these and return the cylinder to the depths of the freezer.

25 dandelion flower heads
130g unsalted butter
100g caster sugar
1 medium egg
1 orange, zest and juice kept separated
200g plain white flour
Pinch of sea salt
150g icing sugar

Preheat the oven to 180°C and discard any green stems from the flower heads and rinse gently under cold running water. Leave to dry, then remove the yellow petals from each flower and place in a bowl to one side. Discard the remains of the flower heads. Next, cream the sugar and butter together until soft and fluffy, then carefully add the egg and all of the orange zest. Mix well, then sift in the flour and salt using a sieve. Lastly, add in the dandelion petals and one tbsp of orange juice, leaving the rest of the juice aside for icing. Combine the whole mixture thoroughly until you have a squidgy dough, adding a little more flour if necessary. Use your hands to take handfuls of dough and form them into balls, then squash each ball down onto a greased baking tray to make a biscuit shape (if your dough is very firm you can also use funky biscuit cutters to create your shapes). Place the tray in the oven for 12 minutes until golden then cool them on a wire rack. Meanwhile, make the icing by sieving the icing sugar into a bowl. Slowly add the orange juice, one tsp at a time, until the icing is runny but not completely out of control. When the biscuits are cool, cover each one with icing (sprinkle with orange zest and dandelion petals for decoration) and leave to set.

Wild Thyme and Sea Buckthorn Vodka

Like sloe gin, alcohol is a great way to capture the complex flavours of our sourest berries and transform them into something entirely drinkable. Sea buckthorn berries are notoriously sour, but the addition of sugar means the resulting concoction is sweet and flavoursome and the thyme brings an aromatic twist much like the basil in a bramble cocktail. Try serving at Christmas with a light, sparkling cider or English sparkling wine like the Hambledon Vineyard's, for a fizzy, yet fragrant, aperitif.

2 litres unflavoured vodka
1kg sea buckthorn berries
500g caster sugar
A few sprigs of fresh thyme

Rinse the buckthorn berries thoroughly under cold running water and gently dry with a tea towel. Lay the berries onto a clean chopping board and, using a heavy rolling pin or similar instrument, tap the berries firmly to burst a few berries and start releasing the juices. Scoop the berries and juices into a sterilised demijohn and add the fresh thyme sprigs and caster sugar. Pour over the vodka and seal the demijohn tightly before shaking gently to dissolve the sugar. Continue to shake once a week for two to three months before straining the vodka through muslin or cheesecloth, then transfer to a warm, sterilised bottle for serving.

Lemon, Marmalade and Poppy-Seed Cake

There is nothing in the world I love more than cake – and I really mean that. This recipe is perhaps my own Frankenstein's monster of cakes, combining the classic lemon drizzle with crunchy poppy seeds, bitter marmalade and the sweet, squidgy petals of mallow flowers. When looking for wild poppies, bear in mind that they only release their seeds when the heads have drooped down and broken the stem. If you want to collect the seeds from unbroken heads, it's good to leave a couple of heads to naturally disperse and ensure the poppies will spread, continue growing and leave a rich habitat for wildlife. That way, we can all enjoy lemon cakes far into the distant future. If you fancy being even more adventurous, grapefruit marmalade also works really well in this recipe.

For the sponge
250g unsalted butter
250g caster sugar
4 eggs, beaten
Zest and juice of 1 lemon
250g self-raising flour, sieved
3 tbsps poppy seeds

For the filling
2 lemons
150g icing sugar
Orange marmalade

For the decoration
Fresh mallow flowers

Preheat the oven to 180°C and grease two 20cm sandwich tins with butter. To make the sponge, cream together the butter and sugar until soft and fluffy. Add the eggs one at a time and mix through slowly, then fold in the flour. Add the lemon zest, juice and poppy seeds and give a final stir. Divide the mixture into the tins and bake for around 20 minutes until lightly golden. When cooked, remove from the tins and leave to cool completely. Meanwhile, make the icing by slowly adding lemon juice to the icing sugar until you have the consistency of single cream. Once the sponges have cooled, place one on a plate. Spread a thick layer of marmalade on top and then drizzle a little icing across. Place the second sponge on top and cover the entire cake with marmalade, then drizzle the remaining icing over the cake and arrange fresh or crystallised mallow flowers to decorate.

Blackberry and Pear Crumble

When the autumn days begin to cool and darken, a fruit crumble is guaranteed to warm the soul and fill the belly. Blackberries taste wonderful when fully ripened and the seeds add a little texture, while the buttery sweetness of the pear creates an earthy flavour when paired with the subtle spice of cinnamon. Cunning foragers will know the location of an orchard from which the pears can be scrumped, although be sure you have permission and avoid trespassing on private land. For grocery shoppers I recommend the Red William variety or any from local farmers' markets. Serve hot with dollops of extra thick cream, preferably after a long October walk in the rain.

400g pears, peeled and sliced
300g blackberries
150g golden caster sugar
¼ tsp cinnamon
200g plain white flour, sieved
125g salted butter, cubed
3 tbsps rolled oats
1 tbsp demerara sugar

Preheat the oven to 190°C and wash the blackberries under cold running water, then leave to dry. Meanwhile, peel the pears and slice into half-moons, removing any tough flesh from the core. Weigh out 25g of the golden caster sugar into a bowl. Take a round baking dish of 20–25cm in diameter and place one layer of pear moons into it, until the bottom is covered and sprinkle lightly with the golden caster sugar. Then add a layer of blackberries and sprinkle once more. Repeat the layers until all the fruit and sugar has been used up and leave the dish aside. In a separate bowl, slice the butter into small cubes and add in the flour. Use your fingers to rub the butter and flour together to create a breadcrumb-like mixture, then add in the rest of the sugar, cinnamon and oats and mix well. Sprinkle over the fruit layers and flatten with the back of a spoon to create a solid, compact layer. Lastly, sprinkle over the demerara sugar to provide a satisfying last crunch. Place the dish in the oven and cook for 35–40 minutes.

Seaweed Frizzles

When I was in my first year of university I lived in a building behind an Asian supermarket; they sold all kinds of intriguing food and drink, including the most delicious fried seaweed crisps. I've been obsessed with them ever since, forever convincing myself the minerals in the seaweed counteract the fat of the frying. When making them myself, I bake them to enrich the flavour and ensure they are healthier (which means you can eat more). You can use any kind of seaweed from this book, including sea lettuce, kelp, sugar kelp, bladderwrack, carragheen, pepper dulse, dulse and laver. They are best served immediately or they may wilt a little.

A few handfuls of seaweed
Olive oil
Smoked paprika
Chilli flakes
Garlic salt

Preheat the oven to 220°C. Rinse the seaweed under cold running water and pat dry with a tea towel. Once dry, chop roughly onto 10cm pieces and place into a large baking tray. Drizzle over a glug of olive oil, then sprinkle over a generous helping each of paprika, chilli and garlic salt. Toss together thoroughly and place the baking tray in the oven for 4–5 minutes until the seaweed has crisped up. Beware! It will burn incredibly quickly if neglected, so take a peek in the oven every 30 seconds or so.

	JANUARY	FEBRUARY	MARCH	APRIL	MAY	JUNE

WOODLAND

	JANUARY	FEBRUARY	MARCH	APRIL	MAY	JUNE
						Elder
						Wild Strawberries
					Lesser Burdock	
						Lime
			Garlic Mustard			
		Sorrel				
				Jewel weed		
Goosegrass						
			Comfrey			
				Common Valerian		
					Herb Bennet	
				Woodruff		
			Ground Ivy			
			Wild Garlic/Ramsons			
					Pignut	
Scarlet Elf Cap						
						Hedgehog Fungus
Oyster Mushroom						

COAST

	JANUARY	FEBRUARY	MARCH	APRIL	MAY	JUNE
			Sea Beet			
				Common Orache		
Sea Purslane						
			Black Mustard			
Wild Cabbage						
				Common Scurvy-grass		
				Lovage		
				Milk Thistle		
		Fennel				
Sea Lettuce						
Kelp or Oarweed						
Sugar Kelp						
Bladderwrack						
Carragheen or Irish Moss						
Pepper Dulse						
Dulse						
Laver						
Sea Buckthorn						

JULY	AUGUST	SEPTEMBER	OCTOBER	NOVEMBER	DECEMBER

WOODLAND

- Hawthorn
- Elder
- Blackberry/Bramble
- Sweet Chestnut
- Walnut
- Oak
- Common Mallow
- Hazel
- Giant Puffball
- Cauliflower Fungus
- Dryad's Saddle

COAST

- Marsh Samphire
- Sea Buckthorn

	JANUARY	FEBRUARY	MARCH	APRIL	MAY	JUNE
HEATHLAND	Common Gorse					
	Juniper					
	Wild Thyme					
					Bog Myrtle	
						Chamomile
MEADOW						Meadowsweet
			Common Nettle			
				Good King Henry		
			Fat Hen			
			Winter Cress or Yellow Rocket			
				Watercress		
			Cuckooflower or Lady's Smock			
				Sweet Cicely		
	Alexanders					
				Ground Elder		
				Hogweed or Cow Parsnip		
					Borage	
				Wild Marjoram		
					Yarrow	
	Chives					
	Wild Parsnip					
	Salsify					
	Dandelion					

	JULY	AUGUST	SEPTEMBER	OCTOBER	NOVEMBER	DECEMBER

HEATHLAND

- Juniper
- Bilberry
- Cranberry
- Rosebay Willowherb
- Bitter Vetch
- Rowan or Mountain Ash

MEADOW

- Guelder Rose
- Blackthorn or Sloe
- Barberry
- Dog Rose
- Crab Apple
- Blackcurrant
- Gooseberry
- Common Poppy
- Hop
- Alexanders
- Sand Leek
- Wild Parsnip
- Salsify
- Goat's Beard
- Field Blewit or Blue Leg

PHOTOGRAPH CREDITS

Bloomsbury Publishing would like to thank the following for providing photographs and for permission to reproduce copyright material within this book. While every effort has been made to trace and acknowledge all copyright holders, we would like to apologise for any errors or omissions, and invite readers to inform us so that corrections can be made in any future editions.

With the exception of the photographs and images listed on the page numbers below, all photographs and illustrations in this book remain © Tiffany Francis.

1 © Shutterstock.com; **8** peteholyoak/iStock; **17** top right saiko3p/iStock, bottom right CribbVisuals/iStock; **21** © Shutterstock.com; **23** bazza1960/iStock; **24** yourmap/iStock; **25** © Shutterstock.com; **26** intst/iStock; **27** top left dmytronasyrov/iStock, top right ShaunWilkinson/iStock, bottom altocumulus/iStock; **30** © Shutterstock.com; **31** Whiteway/iStock; **33** top AdamLongSculpture/iStock, bottom NNehring/iStock; **34** Mantonature/iStock; **37** top right Casara/iStock, bottom left kostik2photo/iStock, bottom right ehaurylik/iStock; **40** Grahamphoto23/iStock; **42** © Shutterstock.com; **43** © Shutterstock.com; **44** ValdisO/iStock; **45** © Shutterstock.com; **46** © Shutterstock.com; **48** agalma/iStock; **50** Val Corbett/Gettimages; **51** Ian_Redding/iStock; **53** mtreasure/iStock; **54** © Shutterstock.com; **55** © Shutterstock.com; **56** Mantonature/iStock; **57** top left © Shutterstock.com, top right MarkMirror/iStock, bottom left Adam88x/iStock, bottom right AlbyDeTweede/iStock; **58** ca2hill/iStock; **59** © Shutterstock.com; **60** © Shutterstock.com; **61** © Shutterstock.com; **66** © Shutterstock.com; **70** AndyRoland/iStock; **72** © Shutterstock.com; **73** © Shutterstock.com; **74** Marcus Webb/FLPA; **75** © Shutterstock.com; **77** © Shutterstock.com; **78** PeakMystique/iStock; **79** top left Mantonature/iStock, top right Whiteway/iStock, bottom left yogesh_more/iStock, bottom right © Shutterstock.com; **80** kongxinzhu/iStock; **81** © Shutterstock.com; **82** Raw_Materials/iStock; **83** © Shutterstock.com; **85** top left © Shutterstock.com, top right fotolinchen/iStock, bottom left Mantonature/iStock, bottom right © Shutterstock.com; **86** © Shutterstock.com; **87** vencavolrab/iStock; **88** JannHulzenga; **89** top MIMOHE/iStock, bottom, triffitt/iStock; **90** NNehring/iStock; **91** YUCELOZBER/iStock; **92** © Shutterstock.com; **93** © Shutterstock.com; **95** © Shutterstock.com; **96** PH2212/iStock; **97** top left © Shutterstock.com; top right zmeel/iStock, bottom Ian_Redding/iStock; **98** © Shutterstock.com; **99** D P Wilson/FLPA; **100** Nick Upton/NPL; **101** BSIP/Gettyimages; **102** Steve Trewhella/FLPA; **103** © Shutterstock.com; **104** ClarkandCompany/iStock; **105** top © Shutterstock.com, bottom georgeclerk/iStock; **116** Magone/iStock; **117** PicturePartners/iStock; **118** Eugenegg/iStock; **119** top and bottom AndreyTTL/iStock; **120** Evgeny Sergeev/iStock; **121** mashabuba/iStock; **125** artistwithcamera/iStock; **126** © Shutterstock.com; **127** top arenysam/iStock, bottom gaiamoments/iStock; **128** Mantonature/iStock; **129** Mantonature/iStock; **130** ziprashantzi/iStock; **131** top Dejan Kolar/iStock, bottom © Shutterstock.com; **132** © Shutterstock.com; **133** Henrik_L/iStock; **148** tverkhovinets/iStock; **149** © Shutterstock.com; **153** top left CatMiche/iStock, top right arinahabich/iStock, bottom left skhoward/iStock, bottom right Lokibaho/iStock; **155** © Shutterstock.com; **156** © Shutterstock.com; **157** © Shutterstock.com; **160** © Shutterstock.com; **161** top left zlikovec/iStock, top right seven75/iStock, bottom left graffoto8/iStock, bottom right Sunlike/iStock; **162** © Shutterstock.com; **163** © Shutterstock.com; **168** Nigel Cattlin/FLPA; **169** Mantonature/iStock; **170** igorbondarenko/iStock; **172** © Shutterstock.com; **173** Enskanto/iStock; **174** Mantonature/iStock; **175** © Shutterstock.com; **176** © Shutterstock.com; **177** © Shutterstock.com; **178** MarkGillow/iStock; **179** top left © Shutterstock.com, top right dabjola/iStock, bottom left Ottochka/iStock, bottom right bkkm/iStock; **180** © Shutterstock.com; **181** © Shutterstock.com; **182** © Shutterstock.com; **183** top StefanieDegner/iStock, bottom BoValentino/iStock; **184** © Shutterstock.com; **185** Mieszko9/iStock; **186** Maica/iStock; **187** © Shutterstock.com; **188** DVB60/iStock; **189** faustasyan/iStock; **190** © Shutterstock.com; **191** ArgenLant/iStock; **192** © Shutterstock.com; **194** © Shutterstock.com; **195** © Shutterstock.com; **196** © Shutterstock.com; **197** CreativeNature_nl/iStock; **198** sonsam/iStock; **199** top Ian Lycett-King/iStock; **200** © Shutterstock.com; **201** © Shutterstock.com;

INDEX